OSPREY COMBAT AIRCRAFT • 3

HELLDIVER UNITS
OF WORLD WAR 2

Gregg M. Taylor

SERIES EDITOR: TONY HOLMES

OSPREY COMBAT AIRCRAFT • 3

HELLDIVER UNITS
OF WORLD WAR 2

Barrett Tillman

OSPREY
AEROSPACE

Front cover
**The Helldiver first won its 'battle
spurs' on Armistice Day, 11
November 1943, when 23 SB2C-1Cs
from VB-17 aboard USS _Bunker Hill_
attacked Japanese naval vessels
sailing in Simpson Harbour, off
Rabaul – they were part of a three
carrier task force sent to bomb the
Japanese stronghold on New Britain.
One destroyer was sunk and three
other ships damaged in the raid, for
the loss of four Helldivers to all
causes. This specially-commissioned
Iain Wyllie painting depicts the
fraught escape made by VB-17's
flight (operations) officer, Lt Bob
Wood, who was chased out of
Simpson Harbour after completing
his diving attack by a division of four
A6M5 Zekes from the 253rd _Kokutai_.
Whilst Wood coaxed maximum
speed from his lumbering Helldiver
at wave-top height, his gunner, Chief
Radioman W O Haynes, Jnr,
succeeded in shooting down two of
the Japanese fighters before he
himself was badly wounded.
Fortunately for the Helldiver crew, a
division of F6F-3 Hellcats from VF-18
then appeared on the scene and
made short work of the remaining
two A6M5s. Once safely back aboard
Bunker Hill, Wood's SB2C-1 was
examined for damage, and no less
than 130 separate bullet holes duly
discovered**

First published in Great Britain in 1997
by Osprey, an imprint of Reed Consumer Books Limited
Michelin House, 81 Fulham Road,
London SW3 6RB
and Auckland, Melbourne, Singapore and Toronto

© 1997 Osprey Publishing
© 1997 Osprey Publishing/Aerospace Publishing Colour Side-views

ISBN 1 85532 689 2

Edited by Tony Holmes
Page design by TT Designs, T & S Truscott
Cover Artwork by Iain Wyllie
Aircraft Profiles by Tom Tullis
Figure Artwork by Mike Chappell
Scale Drawings by Mark Styling

Printed in Hong Kong

ACKNOWLEDGMENTS
The author and publisher wish to acknowledge the assistance provided by Cdr
Harold L Buell, Jim Burridge, Rear Adm Martin D Carmody, Cdr William S
Emerson, Vice Adm Donald Engen, Cdr Mark Fox, Dick Hladky, Robert E.
Holmbeck, Philip Jarrett, Peter Mersky, Norman Polmar, James C Sawruk,
Jerry Scutts, John E Shepard, Jim Sullivan and Capt Robert B Wood.

EDITOR'S NOTE
To make this new series as authoritative as possible, the editor would be
extremely interested in hearing from any individual who may have relevant
photographs, documentation or first-hand experiences relating to combat aircraft, and their crews, of the various theatres of war. Any material used will be
fully credited to its original source. Please write to Tony Holmes at 1
Bradbourne Road, Sevenoaks, Kent, TN13 3PZ, Great Britain.

CONTENTS

DEVELOPMENT AND FLEET SERVICE

Helldiver! The name has become both generic and specific for US Navy dive-bombers of the 1930s and 40s, and was even the title of a motion picture featuring Clark Gable and Wallace Beerey. But the biplane F8Cs flying from USS *Saratoga* (CV-3) in that classic picture were two generations removed from the 275-mph monoplane that sank Japanese warships in the last two years of World War 2.

The Curtiss-Wright company of Buffalo, New York, had a long history of providing military aircraft to the US and friendly governments. Aside from its SB2C, the firm made major contributions to the allied war effort in the form of the Curtiss P-40 series of fighters and the C-46/R5C Commando transport. Immediate predecessor of the SB2C was the streamlined SBC biplane, whose 'genetic' influence would become recognisable in the Helldiver.

The SBC was a limited-production, carrier-based, scout bomber built to the tune of only 258 airframes between 1936 and 1941. In fact, when the first SBC-3 was issued to Scouting Squadron Five (VS-5) on 17 July 1937, it became the last biplane type to join the fleet. Three months later, the Navy's first monoplane carrier aircraft arrived in the form of Douglas' TBD-1 torpedo bomber, which was later christened Devastator.

Such was America's military shortfall on the eve of the Pacific War that

SB2C-1C BuNo 00245 at the Curtiss factory on 20 August 1943. This aircraft was the 45th -1C model, featuring twin 20 mm cannon in the wings rather than the quartet of .50 cal machine guns fitted to the original 'dash one'. The early tricolour camouflage scheme is mated with the mid-war national insignia, which added horizontal bars with a red border around the entire 'star and bars' (*Jim Sullivan*)

Marine Corps squadrons continued to flying SBC-4s throughout 1942 and well into 1943.

Help was painfully slow in coming. A 1938 design competition for a new carrier-based scout bomber drew responses from half a dozen manufacturers. Among others, the more formidable requirements called for an internal bomb bay and overall dimensions allowing two of the aircraft (with wings folded) to ride on an aircraft carrier elevator measuring 40 ft by 48 ft. The Curtiss design team thus faced a nearly insurmountable challenge – designing an airframe with enough internal ordnance and fuel to fit within the confining space of elevators on carriers yet unbuilt.

Spanking new Helldivers are seen soon after having been rolled out of the factory in August 1944. The white block letters on the cowlings reflect the last three digits of the Navy Bureau of Aeronautics number (BuNo) for each aircraft. The sailors in this photograph were part of the Bureau of Aeronautics Representive (BAR) team at the Curtiss plant, their job being to ensure that each machine was ready for acceptance (*Jim Sullivan*)

The result was a short-coupled aeroplane with an oversized empennage to compensate for the aerodynamic problems inherent in the larger configuration. Curtiss' original plan called for a powered gun turret along the lines of that fitted to the Grumman TBF-1 Avenger, but the Bureau of Aeronautics wisely deleted the concept. However, the Helldiver was powered by the Wright R-2600, which was the same engine as successfully fitted to the Grumman/Eastern Avenger. Eventually the problems would largely be resolved, but not without severe penalties in both time and effort, and the aircraft suffering from marginal tactical qualities – especially stability in the dive.

Project engineer on the new scout bomber was Raymond C Blaylock, who had joined Curtiss in 1929 after graduating from the University of Michigan with a degree in aeronautical engineering. With nearly a decade's experience in building military aircraft, Blaylock's credentials included work on the Army's P-6 fighter and the Navy's XF12C-1 and XSBC-1 carrier aircraft.

Blaylock and his team produced results. An order for 370 SB2C-1s was contracted on 15 May 1939, which was a development of mixed fortune for the Curtiss Company. Ordering so many aircraft before the prototype was even completed was extraordinary, but while the Navy contract was welcome, the firm was already committed to building Army Air Corps fighters in Buffalo, New York. Therefore, a new factory complex had to be established in Columbus, Ohio, and these early delays would only be compounded when manufacturing and service problems arose.

During the early part of 1940, aerodynamicists found potential difficulties with the bomber's wing. Wind tunnel tests indicated unacceptably high stall speeds – a condition wholly unacceptable for a carrier aircraft. Therefore, the wing area was increased by nearly 10 per cent, from 385 to 422 ft^2. Aerodynamically-activated leading edge slats were also included as an additional means of improving low-speed stability and control.

From Columbus the original components were shipped to Buffalo to be assembled into the prototype dive-bomber. The XSB2C-1 rolled out of the home plant on 13 December 1940, and was flown for the first time

The fleet's first operational Helldivers were the SB2C-1s of Bombing Squadron 17, seen here aboard USS *Bunker Hill* (CV-17) in the summer of 1943. By that point VB-17 was a consolidation of Air Group 17's bomber and scout squadrons, the 'VS' designation having been abandoned for carrier aircraft. Of interest are the two LSO stripes on the vertical stabiliser of aircraft 'B-19', these serving as a visual reference for the landing signal officer to judge an aircraft's proper attitude as it approached the flightdeck (*Tailhook*)

five days later. Curtiss test pilot Lloyd Childs took the big bomber aloft and returned with marginal enthusiasm. The expected stability problems, though somewhat mollified, had not been eliminated.

The prototype crashed on a test flight only two months later when, in early February 1941, the Wright engine abruptly quit during landing approach. The entire programme suffered a serious setback, not resuming flight tests until early May.

Meanwhile, the Columbus, Ohio, factory was officially opened on 4 December – fortunate timing given events in Hawaii just 72 hours later. Although Curtiss rebuilt the 'X job', it had still not begun Navy acceptance trials when the aircraft's wing failed in flight on 21 December 1941. Test pilot Barton T 'Red' Hulse was able to bail out during a high-G dive recovery, but the prototype was destroyed. By then, of course, America was officially at war and the new scout-bomber's troubled gestation only lengthened.

Meanwhile, an Army Air Force requirement had been released in April 1941 which led to the construction of the A-25A in December 1942. Even without folding wings and catapulting or arresting gear, engineering and production changes led to serious weight penalties, raising empty weight from 7868 lbs to 10,290, or nearly 2500 lbs more.

A production Helldiver first flew on 30 June 1942, barely three weeks after the pivotal Battle of Midway, and four days after the flight of Grumman's prototype XF6F-1 Hellcat. But 'gremlins' caused both the factory and the Navy an endless series of problems, requiring the unusual step of retaining early production aircraft for further development. The first production Helldiver was Bureau of Aeronautics Number (BuNo) 00001, thus beginning the Navy's new serial number series. The previous series had prematurely ended in the 7200-7300 range with Consolidated PB2Y and PBY seaplanes. However, the initial SB2C-1 was lost to wing failure in a dive during January 1943 – the Helldiver programme's third crash in less than two years.

Early SB2C-1s were positioned by two different methods – the 'mechanical mule', as seen in this view taken from 'vulture's row', and the more plentiful muscle power of sailors in the deck crew. This ship is almost certainly *Bunker Hill* or *Yorktown* during work-ups in the summer of 1943 (*US Navy*)

At that stage in its development, the fledgling dive-bomber seemed no closer to joining the fleet than it had been in 1940. Evaluation for the next several months prevented the Navy from authorising SB2C-1s to perform high-speed dives without the use of the marginally-effective flaps. With the addition of service-type equipment such as self-sealing fuel tanks, armour plating and radar, the Helldiver's empty weight rose by a whopping 3000 lbs. Consequently, rated top speed fell from 320 knots (368 mph) to 280 knots (322 mph), while landing speed increased by 10 knots to 79 (91 mph).

A separate 'post-production' line was established at Columbus to install required modifications to newly-finished aircraft – mainly internal fixes and control surface modifications. However, in the spring of 1943 a second programme ('Mod II') of some 800 changes were initiated. Finally, a third set of alterations ('Mod III') were completed in November of that year – the same month that SB2Cs finally entered combat. At some point it must have seemed as if every one of the 15,200 rivets and 45,000 parts in the Helldiver airframe had been replaced.

There were other 'snags' as well, some of which could not be fixed after the design was 'finalised'. One of the lingering problems was the basic configuration, originally dictated by the size of aircraft elevators on many prewar US Navy carriers. Measuring 35 ft 5 in in length, the XSB2C-1 appeared unconventionally short-coupled, especially for a dive-bomber, which aerodynamically required directional stability for bombing accuracy. Eventually the production aircraft grew 15 in to 36 ft 8 in in length, while wingspan diminished about $3^1/2$ inches to 49 ft 8 $^5/8$ in.

A brief divergence from the primary model occurred with the fifth production aircraft. Minus its landing gear, BuNo 00005 was fitted with twin floats and a ventral fin to create the XSB2C-2 seaplane. Some 350 were envisioned at one point, but yet another casualty was sustained when the 'dash two' was lost during water tests and the programme was cancelled.

Whatever the variant of a given aircraft, Curtiss-Wright and other aviation companies faced an endless 'battle' on the home front. Suddenly faced with an urgent need for expanded facilities, thousands of men and women had to be trained to mass-produce complex equipment to tight tolerances. Typically, only one-tenth of the new work force had any aircraft experience, so the company acquired a five-story building in downtown Columbus to teach essential skills to 'Rosie the Riveter' and her male counterparts. Before long, one-third of the Helldiver work force was composed of women from college age upwards. Furthermore, as many as 175 factories in the eastern half of the United States produced SB2C subcomponents and shipped them to Columbus for final assembly.

INTO SERVICE

Initial fleet delivery was made to Scouting Squadron Nine (VS-9) on 15 December 1942 – two years after the prototype's first flight. The last delivery of SB2C-5s occurred in October 1945, totalling 5516 SB2Cs, 834 SBWs from Canadian Car and Foundry and 300 Fairchild SBFs.

The variants with their specific characteristics were:

SB2C-1: 978 of the basic production aircraft with the Wright R-2600-8 engine developing 1700 take-off horsepower for a three-bladed propeller. With a two-stage blower, the R-2600-8 was rated at 1500 hp at 2400 rpm up to 5800 ft, and 1350 hp in high blower up to 13,000 ft.

SB2C-2: experimental floatplane model, never entered production.

SB2C-3: 1112 aircraft powered by the R-2600-20 engine of 1900 horsepower for a four-bladed Curtiss Electric propeller. This engine made use of lighter aluminium cylinder heads. Other differences were perforated dive brakes late in the series, much alleviating the persistent buffeting in fast dives, and use of the APS-4 airborne radar in an underwing housing, deleting need of the original Yagi antenna. Such models were designated SB2C-3E.

SB2C-4: 2045 aircraft powered by same -20 engine, now with a propeller spinner. With rails for eight rockets, offensive armament was increased. The perforated dive brakes introduced late in the 'dash three' model were standard, and the same APS-4 air-search radar was a common fitment in the -4E.

SB2C-5: 970 aircraft with the same -20 engine, but 35 gallons greater fuel capacity. The 'dash five' was not significant during the war years, only entering production in February 1945.

A-25A: 900 fixed-wing dive bombers for the Army Air Force (and eventually the Marine Corps) built at St Louis.

The Canadian-built Helldivers were produced in similar configurations, with SBW-1, -3, -4/4E and -5 variants. SBFs were produced in -1, -3 and -5 models as well, with more than half the Canadian models being 560 'dash three' SBFs and SBWs. Under the Lend-Lease programme, 26 SBWs were sent to Britain for evaluation by the Fleet Air Arm, and although most were delegated to squadrons, none experienced combat service.

Although there were exceptions, the easiest method of distinguishing between Helldiver models was the propeller spinner on three-tone painted SB2C-1s and on the gloss blue 'dash fours'. Tricolour 'dash threes' and gloss blue SB2C-5s usually had the plain prop boss without the spinner. Additionally, SB2C-4s and -5s did not have the Plexiglas window behind the pilot's cockpit.

DIVE-BOMBING

Lt Harold L Buell was among the most experienced dive-bomber pilots in the US Navy during World War 2. His combat deployments included VS-5, VB-10 and VB-2 at Coral Sea, Guadalcanal and through the Central Pacific.

Between combat tours, Buell used every opportunity to impart his knowledge to fledgling aviators. He identified seven portions of a dive-bombing attack, and described each in turn – the approach, break, dive, drop ('shot'), pull-out, withdrawal and rendezvous.

Stability in the dive was the paramount virtue of a dive-bomber, and enormous work went into perfecting the optimum system of dive flaps. The SB2C's original dive brakes, used into the 'dash three' variant, were relatively simple devices – four flaps (two each upper and lower) on each wing, separated at the wing-fold line. They were straight-edged rectangles with a total of 15 holes in each wing's upper set and 41 in the lower set, permitting part of the slipstream to pass through the flaps rather than blanking out the tail. The lower set also doubled as landing flaps.

However, the early configuration of dive flaps caused persistent problems, especially tail buffet which disturbed accuracy. Aerodynamicists determined that the slipstream through, and around, the flaps in a steep dive was disturbed to an unacceptable degree, leading to vibration of the vertical and horizontal stabilisers.

In seeking an improvement, toward the end of the SB2C-3 production run, Curtiss engineers tested a redesigned set of flaps. The new version largely retained the original pattern of larger holes in the flaps, but added scores of much smaller perforations. At the same time, the original straight trailing edge of the upper flaps was crenellated to generate an improved air flow over the tail surfaces. Therefore, SB2C-4s could perform steep, high-speed, dives with improved bombing accuracy. A by-product of the new flaps was somewhat improved aircraft handling in the landing configuration.

LEARNING THE HELLDIVER

Ens Robert E Holmbeck was a fledgling dive-bomber pilot who logged 300 hours in Helldivers in less than a year. In late 1944, his operational training unit, based at Cecil Field, in Jacksonville, Florida, flew SBW-3s and SBF-3, after which he joined the VB-97 pool at NAS Grosse Ile, Michigan, which was equipped with SB2C-4s.

Holmbeck describes the evolution of a 'nugget' aviator into a fleet-ready bomber pilot:

'Most of us had some time in the SBD before we got to Cecil, so we had some experience in fleet-type aircraft. We were all student pilots recently commissioned after finishing flight training. At Cecil Field the operation was pretty much as you would do it in a true squadron. They put ten student pilots together with two instructors, and they all flew together for the entire period as a unit. The chief instructor pilot (IP) led the first division, with the second IP in the lead of the second division;

'We got familiarisation time in the Helldiver, but it didn't take too long, and everybody became pretty proficient. We did navigation, formation, join-ups and break-ups. After that we got into dive-bombing.

'For learning to dive-bomb, they set up at an outlying field from Cecil,

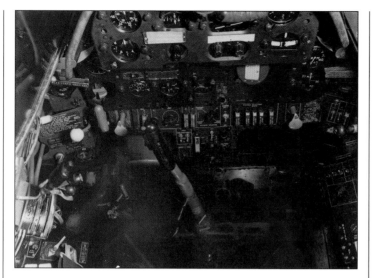

The pilot's cockpit of an SB2C-5, showing flight instruments along the top, fuel and engine gauges on the second tier and mainly armament switches along the bottom. The prominent white knob on the left, ahead of the throttle, is the wing fold handle (*Jim Sullivan*)

behind an instructor flying a simulated attack on a target. But to begin with you had to learn to fly at the exact angle, with 78° being the most efficient. There were observers to coach us into the right angle, whether we were too shallow, too steep or whatever. You started at about 10,000 ft, getting the interval on the aeroplane in front of you, and then pushed over into the dive toward the target. I think the drop altitude was 3000 ft, and we were supposed to be straight and level on the pullout at 1000. The IPs would circle at 1000 to make sure we didn't go too low.

'Next, after 10 to 15 hours of field carrier landing practise, we became comfortable with flying low at slow speed. Then we went out to a ship to become full-fledged carrier pilots. Ours was *Guadalcanal* (CVE-60), out of Mayport, Florida. But it was a small ship that couldn't take many aircraft at one time, so we flew out with six '2Cs, each with another pilot in the back seat to conserve deck space. I rode out with an IP, which was fine with me. Not that I had any qualms about riding with a fellow student, but pilots are all alike – they all want to be the one doing the flying!

'As we approached the deck I remember looking at that little CVE wondering "How does anyone get aboard that?" Unbelievable that in this big, wide, ocean there was such a small rectangular piece of deck that we had to get that big aeroplane onto!

'The IP made the landing, the crew chocked the aeroplane with the engine still running, and I jumped in the front seat for my first take-off. No problem.

'I went around – everything was fine. On the downwind leg you're at 200 ft, do your check list – mixture rich, prop low pitch, gear and flaps down. You unbuckled your parachute from your harness because you're too low to bail out, and if you went in the drink you didn't want the chute strapped on.

'When you were abreast of the stern, you came around on base leg and picked up the LSO's paddles. You focused on him all the way in: too low, slow, high, fast, whatever. When he gave you the cut, you chopped the throttle and pushed over to head right for the deck, then came hard back on the stick so that the aeroplane plopped down in a three-point attitude. Your hook picked up the arresting wire, you rolled out a little, and you'd

The left-hand console featuring throttle quadrant, including mixture, propeller and supercharger controls. Other portside items include the checklist placard, radio equipment and trim tabs for elevators, ailerons, and rudder (*Jim Sullivan*)

The pilot's starboard cockpit console showing electrical panel, tailhook handle, primary radio controls and oxygen regulator. The large circular device with the extended knob is for opening and closing the canopy (*Jim Sullivan*)

made a perfect landing. The aeroplane snagged a wire right where it was supposed to. Man! Your confidence level went up about 1000 per cent. From then on it's a piece of cake – or so you think!

'After three or four landings and things were going very naturally, I came up the groove and everything was normal. The carrier was at a small angle to the wind, not straight down the centre. That day it was 10-15° right, so prop wash was going off to the left.

'When my eyes left the LSO I cut the throttle, heading for the deck and while coming back on the stick, I noticed that the aircraft was drifting left. I was not down the centerline of the deck. The cut signal was mandatory, so I obeyed the cut, but in that fraction of a second I saw that things were not as they should be.

'When I plopped down I pushed on the throttle, still drifting off the deck. Somehow, the tailhook bounced between two arresting wires, or I'd have been in big trouble. And though the wing missed the catwalk, I was headed for the drink. I hauled back on the stick, the throttle was wide open and this thing was settling, settling, settling. It looked to me like I was going in the water, but that machine hung itself on the prop. It didn't settle any farther, so I got the gear up and hung on for dear life.

'I don't know how long it took me to get some decent flying speed, but I got going again, rejoined the pattern and continued on. You couldn't come any closer to going in the drink, but luck was on my side. I made the next landing with no problem and finished the required number, but I often wondered why I didn't get wet. Sometime later I looked back in my logbook and I got a little upset. For some reason the damn fools didn't even give me credit for a touch-and-go-landing!'

'Eventually we learned to sing our very own ditty called "The Helldiver Driver's Song". The author is anonymous:

"Oh Mother, dear mother, take down that blue star.
Replace it with one that is gold.
"Your son is a Helldiver driver; he'll never be 30 years old.
"The people who work for Curtiss are frequently seen good and drunk.
"One day with an awful hangover, they mustered and designed that old
clunk.
"Now the wings are built with precision, the fuselage so strong it won't
fail.
"But who were the half-witted people who designed the cockpit and tail?
"The skipper hates Helldiver drivers and he doesn't think much of that
clunk.
"Each time we fly aboard his carrier, he prays his ship won't be sunk.
"My body lies under the ocean; my body lies under the sea.
"My body lies under the ocean wrapped up in an SB2C!"'

Subsequently Holmbeck received orders to VB-4, the 'Tophatters', at NAS Wildwood, New Jersey, with SB2C-5s. Air Group Four was then assigned to *Tarawa* (CV-40), a brand-new *Essex*-class carrier, for her first deployment, a Western Pacific cruise in 1946.

THE SQUADRONS

From 1943 through to 1945, some 30 Navy bombing squadrons deployed with SB2Cs on combat cruises. There was remarkable continuity in the designations, as Bombing Squadrons One through Twenty and Eighty through Eighty-Eight were all committed to Pacific combat, although not in numerical order. For instance, Bombing 17 initiated the type to combat in November 1943, while VB-15 entered operations aboard *Essex* (CV-9) in May 1944.

Despite the press of wartime, often with only a few months between 'turnarounds', only two air groups made two combat cruises with SB2Cs. The original SB2C squadron, VB-17, returned to the Pacific embarked in the second *Hornet* (CV-12) in early 1945. VB-1 embarked in the second *Yorktown* (CV-10) in May 1944, fought the Marianas battle and then departed in August. Ten months later the reformed VB-1 was back in the Western Pacific aboard *Bennington* (CV-20), remaining in the frontline until after the Japanese surrender. Probably the only other Helldiver unit that came close to a second combat cruise was VB-2, which arrived in *WestPac* only two days after the formal Japanese surrender.

Three other '2C squadrons made split cruises as VB-9, -20, and -80 each flew from two carriers during their combat deployments. The reasons for shifting to other flightdecks were varied, but usually occurred because of battle damage to their original ship, or requirement for refit or repair. Another squadron, Bombing Ten, returned to the US following *Intrepid's* (CV-11) *kamikaze* damage in April 1945, but resumed operations from 'Evil I' just before the end of hostilities.

Despite only two units completing second combat tours, there was an institutional experience level in most SB2C squadrons well beyond the unit records. For instance, Bombing Three, Five, Six, Nine, Ten, Eleven, Twelve and Sixteen had all previously logged wartime deployments with Douglas SBDs, and usually had a smattering of experienced pilots and aircrew the second time out.

The following list details all Navy SB2C squadrons sent to the Western Pacific between November 1943 and August 1945, with their assigned carriers and dates of combat operations:

VB-1	*Yorktown*	May-August 1944
—	*Bennington*	June-September 1945
VB-2	*Hornet*	March-September 1944
VB-3	*Yorktown*	October 1944-March 1945
VB-4	*Bunker Hill*	November 1944
—	*Essex*	November 1944-March 1945
VB-5	*Franklin*	February-March 1945
VB-6	*Hancock*	February-August 1945
VB-7	*Hancock*	September 1944-January 1945
VB-8	*Bunker Hill*	March-October 1944
VB-9	*Lexington*	February-March 1945
—	*Yorktown*	March-June 1945
VB-10	*Intrepid*	March-April, August 1945
VB-11	*Hornet*	October 1944-January 1945
VB-12	*Randolph*	February-May 1945
VB-13	*Franklin*	July-October 1945
VB-14	*Wasp*	May-November 1944
VB-15	*Essex*	May-November 1944
VB-16	*Randolph*	July-September 1945
VB-17	*Bunker Hill*	November 1943-March 1944
—	*Hornet*	February-June 1945
VB-18	*Intrepid*	September-November 1944
VB-19	*Lexington*	July-November 1944
VB-20	*Enterprise*	August-November 1944
—	*Lexington*	November 1944-January 1945
VB-80	*Ticonderoga*	November 1944-January 1945
—	*Hancock*	January-March 1945
VB-81	*Wasp*	November 1944-January 1945
VB-82	*Bennington*	February-June 1945
VB-83	*Essex*	March-September 1945
VB-84	*Bunker Hill*	February-May 1945
VB-85	*Shangri-La*	April-September 1945
VB-86	*Wasp*	March-September 1945
VB-87	*Ticonderoga*	May-September 1945
VB-88	*Yorktown*	July-September 1945
VB-94	*Lexington*	August 1945

VB-81, which deployed with the rest of the air group aboard *Wasp*, began combat operations in November 1944. However, in early January 1945 VF-81 was expanded from 73 to a staggering 90 F6Fs, resulting in removal of the bombing squadron entirely. Torpedo 81 remained aboard with 15 Avengers, but when the fighter complement was reduced to the standard 73, the extra deck space was taken up by two Marine F4U squadrons.

Thirteen fast carriers operated SB2Cs in combat, including *Enterprise*. The other 12 were all *Essex*-class ships. Seven of these embarked three Helldiver squadrons each as their respective air groups cycled through scheduled deployments: *Essex, Yorktown, Intrepid, Lexington, Bunker Hill, Wasp* and *Hancock*.

The following squadron profiles are representative of Helldiver units throughout World War 2, and are presented approximately in chronological order.

BOMBING 17

In mid-1943, Air Group 17 was the Navy's most modern carrier organisation. Lt Cdr Tom Blackburn's Fighting 17 had been the first to receive Vought F4U-1 Corsairs, while the bombing and scouting squadrons were allotted SB2C-1s.

Skipper of VB-17 was Lt Cdr James 'Moe' Vose, an Annapolis graduate and veteran dive-bomber pilot who had flown with VB-8 from *Hornet* (CV-8) at Midway and Santa Cruz. His executive officer was Lt Cdr Geoffrey P Norman, out of the Annapolis class of 1937.

Bombing 17 had 'stood up' with the rest of the air group at NAS Norfolk, Virginia, on 1 January 1943. Originally assigned as commanding officer of the scouting squadron, Vose became CO of VB-17 when, in a Navy-wide reorganisation, the scouts were absorbed into the bombing squadron. The original bomber CO, Lt Cdr W L Blatchford, was reassigned.

The air group's introduction to the Helldiver was unexpected. According to the squadron diarist, less than 60 days after being established, Vose noticed 36 SB2C-1s parked near Hangar LP-4, home of Air Group 17. Curious, Vose wandered over to the neatly-arranged bombers, 'looking like giant squatting bulldogs as they rested on broad landing gears'.

Addressing a mechanic, Vose asked who would receive the Helldivers. To his astonishment, he was told that the Curtisses were reportedly for Scouting and Bombing 17. The rumour was true, as confirmed by the air group commander. Vose read the pilot's manual and began flying the aircraft the next day. Within a week or so his two-dozen pilots were also checked out.

However, the 'bugs' in the sophisticated dive-bomber were numerous

Bombing 17's original complement of Helldiver pilots pose for a group photo outside Hangar LP-4 at NAS Norfolk, Virginia, in mid-1943 (*Capt Robert B Wood*)

and varied. Four aircraft were lost in mid-air collisions, resulting in the death of one pilot. Then in July, the two SB2C squadrons were consolidated into Bombing 17 and Vose inherited full command.

Trouble only continued. Embarking in *Bunker Hill* (CV-17) for a Caribbean shakedown cruise, losses quickly mounted. A, aircraft splashed into the water on launch, and another went straight in during bombing practise, with both men lost. The unit's flight (operations) officer at the time was Lt Robert B Wood who, some 55 years after the cruise, recalled the following aspects of this fraught period in VB-17's history;

'In June 1943 we deployed to the Gulf of Paria, off Venezuela, for operational training. As squadron operations officer, I was responsible for scheduling and training. During this short time at sea it became obvious that the SB2C had major structural problems. On a hard landing, the aircraft buckled just behind the rear seat compartment. In one incident the whole tail section separated and the aircraft, with the pilot and gunner, ended up in the barrier, while the tail section was trapped by the arresting wire.'

Material defects abounded, including tailwheels being lost on impact with the deck. Sentiment leaned toward scrapping the Helldiver in favour of returning to tried-and-true Dauntlesses. However, Vose and the air group commander, Cdr M P Bagdonovich, decided to stay with the big Curtiss and turn it into 'a damn good airplane'.

A major contributor to taming 'The Beast' was Ens Tommy Balzhiser, formerly of Curtiss-Wright. Though granted a draft deferment owing to his important industry work on the Helldiver, Balzhiser wangled his way into the Navy and was commissioned as an Aviation Volunteer Specialist (AV-S) to serve as an SB2C maintenance officer. His intimate knowledge of the aircraft proved invaluable aboard *Bunker Hill* – not only for VB-17, but for the two squadrons which followed in the next two years.

From May to October 1943, VB-17 lost seven aircraft – more than one a month, but probably an acceptable loss rate by wartime standards. Meanwhile, the new *Yorktown* (CV-10) was experiencing similar problems with the Curtiss scout-bomber. Originally equipped with SBD-4s, *Yorktown's* Bombing Squadron Four received SB2C-1s in April 1943, and was joined by VB-6 at Norfolk, Virginia, in May.

The following month, during a shakedown cruise to Trinidad, *York-*

Bombing 17's shakedown cruise had some tense moments. 'Baker Two' lost its empennage upon catching one of *Bunker Hill's* arresting wires on 8 July 1943. Despite this and other problems, VB-17 resisted the suggestion to revert to the Douglas SBD and took the Helldiver into combat before year end (*Jim Sullivan*)

17

The second carrier to receive SB2Cs was USS *Yorktown* (CV-10), which operated Helldivers during early 1943. However, the carrier's skipper, Capt J J 'Jocko' Clark, was so dissatisfied with continuing problems that he arranged for his scout bombers to re-equip with SBD-5s in time for the carrier's deployment to the Pacific that autumn (*US Navy*)

Among the early Helldiver squadrons was VB-8, which formed on the East Coast in July 1943. This photo dates from late that year owing to the red border around the 'star and bars.' The alpha-numeric squadron identification was used only on US-based aircraft assigned to a carrier air group, as such high-visibility markings would have been a liability in combat. Bombing Eight relieved VB-17 aboard *Bunker Hill* in March 1944, and remained aboard until October – one of the longer SB2C deployments of the war (*Tailhook*)

town's skipper, Capt J J 'Jocko' Clark, finally tired of trying to cope with the unending technical and operational difficulties. Having lost some aircraft whose tails fell off in flight, Clark refused to keep SB2Cs aboard. While en route to Pearl Harbor in mid-July, *Yorktown's* scout-bomber unit was redesignated VB-5 after reverting to SBD-5 Dauntlesses. The squadron completed a successful combat deployment between September 1943 and March 1944. Bombing Five finally converted to Helldivers and took them to the Western Pacific for an abbreviated cruise before *Franklin* (CV-13) was severely damaged by a *kamikaze* in March 1945.

BOMBING EIGHT

Although the original Bombing Squadron Eight had flown from USS Hornet (CV-9) at Midway and Santa Cruz, when the squadron reformed in 1943, Lt Cdr Ralph Shifley's unit was composed almost wholly of 'nugget' aviators. Among the half-dozen exceptions were Lts Martin D 'Red' Carmody and Leslie Ward, both of whom were experienced SBD pilots from Air Group 10 aboard Enterprise (CV-6) in 1942-43. With only a five-month 'turn-around' period, a frantic schedule was adopted to qualify 45 pilots and aircrewmen. Summarised Carmody, 'We preached teamwork, teamwork, teamwork'.

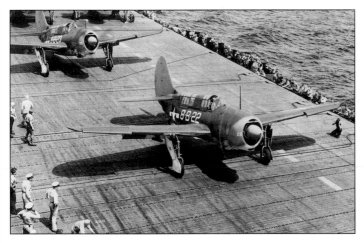

Bombing Eight Helldivers conduct carrier qualification during work-ups in the Atlantic. Note that '8-Baker-22' has begun its take-off from the 490-ft marker, which indicates the distance from that point of the decking to from the forward edge of the flightdeck. With 25 to 30 knots of relative wind over the bow, successful launches could be conducted in such short spaces (*US Navy*)

VB-8 did carrier qualifications in SBD-5s, then got SB2C-1s at Fentress, Virginia – a 3000-ft airstrip on the Atlantic coast. The transition was delayed owing to the slow arrival of Helldivers, increased maintenance problems, and the necessity for aircrew and mechanics to adjust to new equipment. Apparently Bombing Eight was responsible for the Helldiver's unofficial name, when a junior aviator returned to the ready room, ashen-faced after a harrowing landing and blurted out, 'My god, what a beast.'

There were problems upon problems. So many Helldivers were lost in the water that VB-8 established its own fraternity, the 'Beast Dunkers Association'. There was quite a bit of dunking going on – five in December during transit west aboard *Intrepid*, and another while in Hawaii in January, before relieving VB-17 aboard *Bunker Hill* in March. That month the squadron lost 10 aeroplanes to all causes, largely during strikes at the Palaus. In April four more went down during the second Truk strike, and a whopping 17 SB2Cs were lost in June, which included those downed during the strike on the Japanese fleet west of Saipan. Five more in July and one final loss in August raised the unit total to 43 Helldivers in nine months – about 115 per cent of the authorised aircraft strength.

Aircrew losses were also high. From reorganisation through training and completion of the *Bunker Hill* cruise, VB-8 lost 38 men – 19 pilots and 19 radiomen-gunners. Of these, 35 were killed in combat, or operational accidents in the war zone.

Some of the hazards struck the fliers as decidedly bizarre. For instance, prior to strikes on Hollandia, New Guinea, aircrews were briefed on what to expect if forced down. Recalled Red Carmody, 'They told us about the alligators in that area – it scared me more than any thought of the Japanese!'

Still, the challenge of carrier aviation and the companionship of a tightly-knit squadron kept morale up. Carmody felt that typical young American males usually adapted well to such an environment, given good leadership. 'It was like sports in a way, working up the plays and developing a confident attitude.' Carmody, who later commanded US carrier operations in the Tonkin Gulf, led a 'wing' of 12 Helldivers while serving as executive officer of VB-8. His 64 missions covered a wide variety of operations – anti-shipping strikes, ground targets, radio relays, chaff dispensing (gunners dumped bales at Yontan) and rescue support.

The latter mission saw the Helldivers lend their weight to an exceptional rescue when Fighting Eight pilot Lt(jg) John Galvin bailed out at Wolei Atoll in the Caroline Islands. Courageous submarine skipper, Cdr Sam Dealey, nosed USS *Harder* onto the reef and put ashore a rubber raft to fetch back the future ace. Meanwhile, SB2Cs suppressed Japanese gunfire on either side of the beach. It was one of the most daring rescues of the Pacific War.

19

Six Helldivers are seen on a training flight in the United States during December 1943. They may be from VB-20, which had only recently been formed at San Diego with 18 SBD-5s and 9 SB2C-1s (*Jim Sullivan*)

Photography also became a Helldiver mission. From his first combat deployment in 1942-43, Carmody firmly believed 'You can't believe your own eyes – or anyone else's!' Therefore, VB-8 issued a K-25 camera to the radioman-gunner in each division leader's aircraft.

Near the end of its cruise, VB-8 received SB2C-3s, which were welcomed by the pilots. 'Red' Carmody recalls;

'I took 12 pilots by whaleboat over to the USS *Barnes* (CVE-20) to fly them back to the *Bunker Hill*. Because of the crowded flightdeck conditions, we all experienced our first catapult shot. The catapult was only about 80 ft long and the black powder gave us one hell of a launch. To make room for the new "Beasts", the old were stripped and pushed over the side of the *Bunker Hill*. I think we flew the rest of our -1Cs to Eniwetok and returned to the carrier with the rest of the "dash threes". The four-bladed prop helped us to accelerate faster on take-off.'

BOMBING TWO

Bombing Squadron Two joined its parent air group at NAS Quonset Point, Rhode Island, in July 1943. Formed from two pre-existing units, VB-2 was led by Lt Cdr G B Campbell. However, none of the three senior officers (CO, executive officer and flight officer) had combat experience. Therefore, Commander Naval Air Forces Atlantic transferred in two Pacific veterans – Lt Harold L Buell and Lt(jg) Vernon Micheel. 'Hal' Buell was probably unique in having been present at each of the 1942 carrier battles, and 'Mike' Micheel had flown at Midway.

Campbell's pilots gained an identity for themselves as 'The Sea Wolves'. On short notice they traded their Dauntlesses for Helldivers at Hilo, Hawaii, in February 1944. The original contingent was 21 SB2C-1s in the 00030-50 serial range.

By then Hal Buell was third in the squadron's seniority, serving as flight (operations) officer. He felt that, despite the Curtiss' speed and greater firepower, 'the disadvantages far outweighed the plusses' compared to the Dauntless. 'To take the majority of VB-2 pilots out of the only combat aircraft they had flown. . . then put them in a "Beast" and launch them on a mission, was imprudent.' Still, the decision stuck, and VB-2 had only about 30 days to assimilate its new weapon.

Aboard *Hornet* (CV-12), and most other CV-9 class carriers through most of 1944, the fighter squadron usually had side numbers 1 through 40, with the bombers running 41 to 76 or so. They flew six-aircraft divisions, each composed of two three-aircraft sections. In VB-2, Lt Cdr Campbell's division had side numbers 41 to 46, Buell's division had 47 to 52, Lt JR Smith's team was 53 to 58, Lt Lyle Felderman's was 59 to 64, Lt Micheel's was 65 to 70 and Lt(jg) Jesse Bamber's division was 71 to 76.

A shaken pilot is helped from his **SB2C-1C** after a disastrous landing aboard *Hornet* (CV-12) on 7 January 1944. Note that the airframe broke at the production joint in the rear cockpit. This event occurred during a carrier qualification (CQ) period performed just five weeks after the ship had been commissioned (*Jim Sullivan*)

As flight officer, Hal Buell attempted to fly every new aircraft assigned to the squadron. He recalls, 'My logbook indicates that I flew 16 SB2C-1s, 28 SB2C-1Cs and 10 SB2C-3s – a total of 54 different aircraft on approximately 100 flights between March and October 1944 on our war cruise.'

Bombing Two broke into combat on 30 March 1944 with attacks on Peleliu Island in the Palaus, 500 miles east of the Philippines. The Helldivers sank a transport on their first mission and later bombed facilities at an airfield. However, one aircraft and crew were lost on each mission.

Subsequent operations included supporting the Hollandia, New Guinea, landings prior to the Marianas campaign in mid-June. During the dusk strike on the Japanese fleet on 20 June, VB-2 played a major role in the attack on Vice Adm Ozawa's northern carrier group, but suffered heavy losses – 12 aircraft and three fliers.

Air Group Two departed *Hornet* on 29 September (early in the Philippines campaign), being relieved by Air Group 11. During VB-2's last month of combat, the squadron received several 'dash threes'. Throughout its combat cruise, Bombing Two owned dozens of Helldivers to maintain 36 operational at any one time. Indeed, no fewer than 22 were written off in June alone. Combat and operational attrition resulted in a total of 47 being lost or replaced during the deployment from March to September 1944

From a nominal allotment of three-dozen dive-bombers, at least 24 were required to be operational. That was enough to provide the VB contribution to two full deck loads during a day of sustained operations – 12 bombers were usually escorted by 12 fighters, along with 6 to 10 Avengers. However, in addition to two or three deck load strikes, a day's flight schedule also required a few SB2Cs to perform anti-submarine patrols. The flight schedule was driven by aircraft availability, and a high-maintenance aircraft like the Helldiver kept engine and airframe mechanics working 12- to 14-hour days.

BOMBING 11

Bombing Squadron 11 was similar to many Navy scout-bomber units because it flew both Douglas Dauntlesses and Curtiss Helldivers. However, the 'Pegasus' squadron was unusual in that it flew SBD-3s from Guadalcanal before finally achieving carrier duty. Originally intended as part of a replacement air group for the first *Hornet* (CV-8), which was sunk in October 1942, VB-11 reached the Solomon Islands in April 1943 and remained at 'Cactus' until that July. Flying SBD-3s, the squadron logged numerous shipping strikes into the central and northern Solomons.

Fittingly, Air Group 11 reported aboard the second *Hornet* (CV-12) in the fall of 1944, relieving Air Group Two.

Lt Edwin M Wilson had flown SBDs at Guadalcanal and remained with VB-11 for a second combat deployment with SB2C-3s. His comparison of the two types is based on considerable experience in both;

'I have been asked many times which I preferred, the Douglas SBD Dauntless or Curtiss SB2C Helldiver. I liked them both, as they brought me back alive. The SBD was easier to handle in a dive, to aim, and to keep the "ball" centred. If you were in a skid when you released your bomb, the same skid would be on your bomb, thereby reducing chances of a hit. The SBD could also take more flak damage – it was more rugged.

'The SB2C had more speed and range, and it carried more armament. I especially liked the 20 mm cannon in each wing, which alternated tracer, armour-piercing and explosive shells. I did a lot of damage with those guns. As I would make my vertical dive, usually from 10,000 to 12,000 ft, I would fire the cannon all the way down until I released my bomb at about 2000 ft. As in the SBD, we would black out on pull-outs, pulling about five to ten Gs every time. I once pulled 13 Gs in an SB2C, so it, too, was rugged – all it did was ripple the top of the wings, which were easily changed. You would pull negative Gs pushing over into your dive. The most negative Gs that I ever pulled were six. Both negative and positive Gs were recorded by an accelerometer. I think we dive-bomber pilots had "the right stuff", even though at times much of our blood was in our feet!'

Wilson had occasion to test the Helldiver's ruggedness under surprising conditions:

'I never knew why the SB2C had such a large vertical stabiliser and rudder, as I once flew it without them. On 6 November 1944 I led a strike on

Another victim of *Hornet's* 7 January CQ period was this VB-15 Helldiver, which lost most of its 'tail feathers' to a following aircraft whose propeller left an indelible impression. It appears that the radioman-gunner's cockpit is empty – a normal precaution when fledgling aviators tried their first carrier landings in unfamiliar aircraft (*Jim Sullivan*)

Clark Field, on Luzon. Just as I closed my dive brakes and pulled the stick back into my gut, blacking out, I heard a loud explosion. The one good thing about radio and engine noise was that it kept you from hearing anti-aircraft shells exploding. The "word" was that if you heard an explosion, it would be the last thing you would ever hear. So, as soon as I finished my pullout and my vision returned, I asked my gunner, Harry Jespersen, what happened. "Mr Wilson", he replied, "we have no tail." Apparently, when a 40 mm shell exploded, it blew the vertical stabiliser and rudder off at the fuselage.

'Fortunately, I had pulled out in the direction of our task force, so I turned the lead over and kept the aircraft level. Figuring there must have been a purpose for that large vertical surface, I did not drop a wing or attempt a turn. I set her down by a picket ship, the destroyer USS *Mansfield* (DD-728). I landed into a wave that broke over us. I immediately jumped out on the wing to help "Jes" get the raft out, which was in a tube between us, opening into the rear cockpit. He was still landing with his arms over his face and head! We had no shoulder straps or hard helmets, so we had to protect our heads. When I tapped his shoulder, he was really startled – he must have thought I was St Peter.

'Standing on the wing, we inflated the raft and stepped aboard. The SB2C stayed afloat for about 45 seconds. As there was a 40-knot sea, we had a rough time getting aboard *Mansfield*. One minute we would be looking down on it and the next looking up at it. We finally got aboard. My first "sea command" as CO was a two-man raft, and it was of too short a duration to go to my head.

'Two days later, *Mansfield* swung us over to *Hornet*. It took a little longer than usual. I told Cdr Braddy (*Mansfield's* skipper) that *Hornet* usually swapped 20 gallons of ice cream for a returned Navy pilot and 10 gallons for a Marine pilot. So, he would not release me until he got his 20 gallons of ice cream!'

BOMBING 19

Like VB-2, Bombing 19 had little time to switch from Dauntlesses to Helldivers before entering combat. Lt Cdr Richard McGowan's squadron relied upon war-weary SB2C-1s for transition training. There was precious little opportunity for pilot checkouts and familiarisation of mechanics with a larger, more complex, aircraft than the SBD.

One Bombing 19 aviator summarised the squadron's initial batch of Helldivers by saying, 'Their physical condition reflected their BuAer numbers like 00037 and 00039. The hydraulic system was a nightmare arrangement and did not enhance our opinion of the airplane one iota'. Another pilot merely wrote, 'What a big, heavy, sluggish bastard it is!'

While hastily learning the Helldiver, VB-19 continued flying SBD-5s for some training missions. These included towing target sleeves for air-to-air gunnery practise, which led to a philosophical controversy among the junior officers. Donald Engen, later a vice admiral and director of the National Air and Space Museum, reflected, 'We ensigns reasoned that since we were the most junior, we should have the most gunnery practise, but the fact of life was that lieutenants did not like to tow and neither did the lieutenants (junior grade), and so we ensigns towed and we towed.'

Finally, in May the squadron received 35 new SB2C-3s at Maui. Pilot

and aircrew morale improved considerably, as most fliers regarded the new model with far greater enthusiasm than the clapped-out 'dash ones'. Pilots enjoyed learning to operate radar in both the search and attack modes, prompting speculation as to how many inert bombs struck 'that big rock off the end of Molokai'. Night bombing was conducted in Hawaii, during which one pilot landed and noticed he had made the entire flight with his wing-fold mechanism in the unlocked position.

Donald Engen compared the two models of Helldiver thusly;

'The SB2C-3 was a great improvement over the SB2C-1. It was a delight to fly. In mid-June we flew to USS *Franklin* (CV-13), which was deploying westward to the war, for carrier qualifications in the SB2C. Each pilot made four landings. On 20 June we were alerted that we would be moving to the Western Pacific as a 30-aeroplane squadron instead of our current 36. We would retain our current complement of pilots and aircrew. At that time I had 18 flights and four carrier landings in the SB2C-3, but really felt tactically ready.'

Typical of the overall Helldiver experience level in VB-19 was Ens William S Emerson. When he launched on his first combat mission from *Lexington* (CV-16) on 18 July, he had nearly 800 flight hours, but fewer than 100 in SB2Cs, including just seven carrier landings 'in type' and one catapult shot. However, the 'dash three' imparted greater confidence than the SB2C-1s previously flown. Recalled Emerson, 'I felt pretty good about the SB2C-3, particularly after having experienced the -1 and -1C. That four-bladed prop and the 200 extra horses made a big difference!'

From July to November Emerson flew 25 missions in 19 different aircraft, the most being four flights in BuNo 18662. He was shot down on his 10th mission (a strike against Iwo Jima on 4 August 1944), and with his gunner spent 26 days aboard a rescue submarine. It says much about

Thirteen of *Hornet's* dive-bombers are seen ranged aft on the flightdeck on 15 February 1944. Two of them, numbers 2 and 21, show evidence of rudder damage, which was probably caused during aircraft handling accidents. Despite such problems, Bombing 15 compiled a superior combat record while flying from *Essex* later that year (*Jerry Scutts*)

the state of training of wartime naval aviators that upon rejoining *Lexington* in early October, Emerson was catapulted on an anti-submarine patrol without having touched a stick in eight weeks! Another bonus was belated knowledge that in his absence he had been promoted to lieutenant, junior grade.

BOMBING 83

Near the end of the war, Bombing Squadron 83 aboard *Essex* summarised its experience with the SB2C-4/4E;

'The basic aeroplane is good, but hampered by inept mechanical design. Past difficulties often have been corrected at the expense of adding more weight and further complexity. Many detailed parts of the plane are unduly complicated, unreliable and difficult to work on. Despite all this, the plane performs well and is generally well suited to carrier operations and the service it is used for. Maintenance of later models is better than earlier models. Availability, 93 per cent for the present cruise, is considered to have been excellent. Many minor changes formerly made by operating squadrons are now incorporated in the SB2C-4E, but there are still a number of changes which are highly desirable and which, it is felt, should be incorporated in future production.

'All but one of the pilots in the squadron believe that the rear seat man is now, with adequate fighter protection, an unnecessary appendage and just an added responsibility. They would prefer a single-seat SB2C, which should have better flight characteristics and a greater bomb load. If this change were made, the fuselage should be faired straight aft of the cowl, permitting a bubble canopy for the pilot and the necessary visibility aft. All rear-seat equipment, hatch, and turtleback would naturally be eliminated and a better arrangement of radio gear would be possible. The bomb bay could be extended aft and the load increased in proportion to wight removed and better flight characteristics made possible.'

Commenting specifically upon the airframe and flight controls, the report continued;

'Present models are characterised by far better workmanship than earlier versions, and the general ruggedness of the plane has been increased as a consequence.

'Wing dimpling at the main spar is not evident in the -4E. Several wings have been wrinkled at the slot cut-out in pulling out of clean dives, but this has not been serious as high velocities or extreme acceleration have not been reached. It is felt the wing is perfectly satisfactory for dive- bombing with flaps, but is not strong enough for clean, prolonged, dives as in high-speed rocket runs.

'The present SB2C is stable enough to fly comfortably, and control forces would be satisfactory were it not for the friction encoun-

Unlucky 13 – Bombing Squadron 13 sustained this deck crash aboard the escort carrier *Charger* on 20 February 1944. As deck hands work to retrieve the Helldiver from the catwalk, its tailhook still grasps the arresting wire to the right of the photo (*Jim Sullivan*)

A plane director shows the way up the flightdeck to the pilot of an SB2C-3 which has just recovered aboard ship. He has taxied forward over the steel-cable barriers, which now raise behind him to protect parked aircraft from damage in the event of a landing accident (*Jerry Scutts*)

tered in all stick movements. This is particularly true of all aileron controls, which are very tiring. Now that the instability of the earlier models has been removed, the control feel could be improved by removing the elevator counterweight installed at the base of the stick.

'The manufacturer provides no means of securing the trunnion pivot screws of the tab mechanisms, except an elastic stop jam nut which is not adequate. As manufactured, the trunnions will jump out of place and move the tab to the extreme position – a very dangerous condition, particularly in dives. This squadron safety-wires the pivot screws by passing safety wire through the screwdriver slot. A cotter pin would be a better arrangement.'

In other categories, VB-83 had high praise for the Wright R-2600-20 engine, and noted that previous trouble with the Curtiss Electric propeller was 'virtually eliminated' in the 'dash four'. More specifically, the squadron concluded, 'Engine performance has been good and probably more reliable than the (P&W) R-2800. Fuel consumption has been low, as all pilots have been thoroughly indoctrinated into low RPM, high manifold pressure and a lean mixture. Overall fuel consumption has averaged about 60 gallons per hour'.

BOMBING 98 AND THE RAGS

As replacement aircrews went to the fleet in growing numbers, a means was needed to provide them with a 'finishing school' prior to 'graduation'. The method selected was the replacement air group (RAG), organised like an embarked air group with appropriate bombing, fighting, and torpedo squadrons.

The first of these was Air Group 100 at NAS Barbers Point, Hawaii, with VB-100 established on 1 April 1944. It was followed by Air Group 99 in the Marshall Islands area in mid-July. VB-99 was eventually based at Majuro and Eniwetok Atolls, before settling in the Marianas. While Air Group 100 conducted advanced training in Hawaii, it and CVG-99 were increasingly employed as 'ready service lockers' for replacement pilots and aircrews.

Two 'stateside' RAGs were established in the fall of 1944 – Air Group 97 at various bases in the eastern United States, and Air Group 98 on the West Coast. Because so many air groups were formed on the East Coast for eventual service 'somewhere in the Pacific', Bombing 97 stood up at Wildwood, New Jersey, on 1 November. Originally equipped with 17 F6F-3 Hellcats merely for proficiency flying, the squadron soon received SB2Cs. A detachment was formed at NAS Grosse Ile, Michigan, for carrier qualification purposes on the Great Lakes, using the paddle-wheel training carriers *Wolverine* (IX-64) and *Sable* (IX-81).

VB-98 was the West Coast replacement training squadron for fledgling dive-bomber crews. Established at Ventura, California, on 28 August 1944, Bombing 98 originally had 14 SB2C-3s and 4 SBD-5s. The task of training as many as 300 pilots or gunners at one time proved a significant challenge.

However, Capt John Crommelin, the West Coast aviation training officer, had a solution. To organise VB-98, he tapped Lt Cdr James D Ramage, a two-tour *Enterprise* veteran and former commanding officer of Bombing Ten. 'Jig Dog' proved equal to the task.

Reporting to NAAS Ventura that August, Ramage found the CAG was Cdr Bruce Weber, formerly CO of VF-34. The air group was formally established on 7 November 1944, with VF and VT-98 also sharing facilities at Ventura County Airport. However, with insufficient room, few aircraft, and no permanent mechanics, other arrangements were clearly needed.

Therefore, Ramage and his executive officer, Lt Lou Bangs, moved the squadron to NAAS Los Alamitos in early December. Realising that combat knowledge was crucial to the success of his training mission, Ramage arranged for two *Enterprise* shipmates to join VB-98 – Lts Martin Carmody and Frank West. Among them, the handful of instructors devised a 60-hour training syllabus supported by the maintenance personnel of Carrier Air Service Unit 33.

But even this new arrangement stretched available resources. Carrier landing practise was done at a nearby Army landing strip, with other training done at Thermal and Twenty-Nine Palms, both in California, plus weapons employment in the Salton Sea. Finally, Ramage appropriated an FM-2 Wildcat fighter to speed his rounds among three or four different facilities.

Eventually VB-98 was able to begin carrier qualifications for its trainees. The duty 'flattop' was USS *Matanikau* (CVE-101), which provided not only daylight 'CQ' but enabled tyro bomber pilots to make nocturnal passes, getting a feel for the deck at night.

By July 1945 Bombing 98 had 26 SB2C-4s and -5s at 'Los Al' and Thermal Field. The East Coast bombing RAG, VB-97, boasted 37 SB2C-4Es at Grosse Ile, Michigan, and Wildwood, New Jersey, plus a half-dozen Corsairs.

Meanwhile, in the Pacific, VB-100 at NAS Barbers Point owned just 18 'dash fours' or 'fives' – a reflection of the diminished number of Helldiver crews embarked in combat carriers. The replacement pool on Saipan, VB-99, flew 26 SB2Cs or SBWs. Of the four RAGs, three were disestablished almost immediately after the war – CVG-99 in September 1945, CVG-100 in February and CVG-97 in March 1946. However, CVG-98 survived as Air Group 21, which lasted until August 1947.

An SB2C pilot prepares to receive the 'cut' signal from the LSO. Carrier qualification was the most demanding phase of operational training for naval aviators, and during World War 2 there was little margin for error in the days before angled decks. Pilots said there were only three possible results to an approach – a wave-off, an arrested landing or a major accident! Note the plane guard destroyer sailing in the wake of the carrier (*Jim Sullivan*)

INTO COMBAT

Ironically, Bombing Squadron 17 initiated the SB2C to combat on Armistice Day, 11 November 1943. Six days before, a small task force composed of *Saratoga* (CV-3) and the light carrier *Princeton* (CVL-23) had struck the Japanese naval-air bastion at Rabaul, New Britain, and damaged seven warships. Now a far larger follow-up strike was underway, with four other carriers besides *Bunker Hill*. Lt Cdr Vose's aircrews regarded their combat debut with some trepidation, as Rabaul was the major enemy base in the South-west Pacific.

Intelligence on the target was spotty. With only 24 hours notice, planners and squadron commanders worked hard at developing a strike plan to cover the major contingencies. Of Rabaul itself, the salient feature was a volcano that had erupted in 1936.

Tailhooks locked down, two Helldivers from VB-17 maintain station in the landing pattern over *Bunker Hill* whilst squadronmates land back aboard the ship following the Rabaul raid on 11 November 1943 (*Capt Robert B Wood*)

After reveille at 0330, the *Bunker Hill* fliers enjoyed a steak breakfast. Following a final briefing in Ready Rooms Five and Six, the bomber squadron received advice from two sources. Vose reminded his men to 'Stay in formation', while the ship's chaplain quoted the Book of Ecclesiastes. 'There is a time to pray and a time to fight', adding, 'Go get 'em!'

Vose led 23 Helldivers off the deck, flying with W E Stucker as his gunner in aircraft 'B-4' (a further eight Helldivers remained on the carrier as a standby force for either a secondary attack or to undertake an Intermediate Air Patrol). Stucker had offered to buy his skipper a cigar in exchange for a hit on a Japanese ship. However, the mission started badly as one bomber (coded 'B-27') went into the water, taking Lt(jg) R L Gunville (who was initially within the standby force) with it. His gunner, E S Burrow, was rescued by a destroyer.

Winding its way through thunderclouds reaching 12,000 ft, Air Group 17 found Simpson Harbour full of Japanese shipping. Mitsubishi A6M5 Zekes were airborne, but Fighting 18 Hellcats met them, beginning a prolonged dogfight.

Vose decided upon a two-division attack in order to spread as much damage as possible. Leading the first division, he proceeded ahead, while a cruiser in the outer harbour was assigned to Lt Cdr Jeff Norman, the executive officer, in 'B-31'. Co-ordinating with the Avengers of VT-17, the XO's division opened its bomb bays, split its dive flaps, throttled back and nosed over. Rear-seatmen saw the first two bombs either hit the cruiser or explode close alongside, lifting the bow out of the water.

Meanwhile, Vose continued with his half of the squadron until the Helldivers broke into clear air. Sighting destroyers and cruisers manoeuvring offshore, he took four aircraft down on the nearest of two cruisers and dropped from 1300 ft. His 'thousand pounder' exploded alongside, quickly followed by three direct hits by Lt(jg) Palmer ('B-23'), Lt Martin (''B-12') and Lt(jg) Gerner ('B-16').

Vose's second flight, led by Lt Robert Friesz ('B-2'), selected a destroyer. Friesz pressed his dive to the limit, only releasing at 800 ft. He sensed the explosion as his 'Beast' was rocked by concussion, and later learned that he had detonated depth charges on the ship's stern. Other pilots watched the destroyer lose way, burning, while two other warships were also hit.

The bombers were relatively unhindered during their withdrawal – the Zeke pilots were for the most part content to pace the Helldivers, as if sizing up the strange new aircraft. However, three or more Mitsubishis stalked Lt Chinn ('B-5'). In a running battle, Chinn's gunner, De Graff, kept the fighters at bay, though accidentally perforated his aircraft's vertical stabiliser in the process.

Twenty minutes after the carrier aircraft attacked, the strike was completed. One destroyer was sunk and three ships damaged in this effort.

During their time over Rabaul, VB-17's gunners shot at half a dozen or more Zekes, claiming three destroyed and one damaged. Later in the day, returning from an anti-submarine patrol, Ens WH Harris ('B-21') and Radioman D W Thompson engaged Aichi D3A dive-bombers attacking the US task force and shot down one 'Val' and damaged another. Back aboard ship, 'Bucky' Harris was accosted by some Hellcat pilots who insisted that shooting down enemy aircraft was their exclusive province.

This shot of VB-17 veteran Bob Wood shows him in the cockpit of an F6F-5 of VF-92, a unit he commanded in 1944-45 (*Capt Robert B Wood*)

Harris was apparently unimpressed with their argument, for he later became an ace by destroying four more Japanese aircraft while flying Corsairs from *Essex* in 1945.

The squadron lost four SB2Cs during the day, including Gunville's on take-off, one each to flak and fighters, and one that recovered but was jettisoned with extensive battle damage.

Lt Robert B Wood (in 'B-6') led the second four-aircraft division, which was positioned to the left of Lt Cdr Vose's lead flight during the first strike. Here, he recounts his memories of the day;

'It was a beautiful day when we launched – clear blue sky, cloudless, with unlimited visibilty. *Bunker Hill* sortied 27 Hellcats, 23 Helldivers and 19 Avengers. The other two carriers launched a maximum strike effort. The three air groups rendezvoused around the ships, with the Hellcats flying cover about 5000 ft above the bombers and torpedo aircraft. We climbed en route to 21,000 ft. On the attack run we went into a 70° dive, released at about 5000 ft and pulled level at about 3000 ft. As we approached the harbour of Rabaul, we could see that we had a number of lucrative targets – major capital ships of the Imperial Navy.

'Skipper Vose assigned each of the six divisions a specific ship to attack. My division was assigned a cruiser. Each Helldiver was carrying four 500

Helldiver off to war – an SB2C-1 prepares for a deck-run take-off during operations in early 1944. Note that the launch officer, with the checkered flag, is prepared for the worst – he wears an inflatable life belt around his waist and a Colt M1911 .45-cal pistol in an issue holster (*US Navy*)

-lb armour-piercing bombs, and my division had at least four direct hits on the cruiser, along with enough near misses to leave her sinking.

'On the completion of our dive, we were to descend to sea level and rendezvous at the harbour entrance for the return flight to the ship. However, as I was descending and proceeding to the rendezvous, I came under attack by a division of four Japanese Zekes, and as I continued my descent to the water my gunner, Chief Radioman W O Haynes, Jnr, shot down two of the Zeros before he was seriously wounded. A division of Hellcats came by and despatched the other two fighters, and I carried out that well known manoeuvre of getting out of there at "max" speed.

'I knew we were pretty badly shot up because the Zeros had made at least three runs on us, and I had lost communication with Haynes. It turned out that he had been hit in the jaw by a 7.7 mm bullet, which had ricocheted off the protective armour plate in the rear cockpit, and thus prevented him from talking. However, he did give an "Ok" in Morse code using his mike button, so I knew that he was alive.

'After the air battle the return flight to *Bunker Hill* was uneventful. Haynes had a bullet lodged in his jaw, which was not life threatening, and from which he recovered. My SB2C had 130 bullet holes in it, with one string of bullets into the leak-proof gas tank between Haynes and me!

'The attack on Rabaul was the baptism in combat for the *Bunker Hill*, its embarked air group and the SB2C Helldiver. Each of the crews on the attack had a story to tell. There were a number of close calls, and some did not make it back, but all hands measured up to the job to be done.'

Nearly two years after Pearl Harbor, the Helldiver was in the war.

Over the next four months Bombing 17's aircrew flew a variety of missions. They supported Marines at Tarawa, attacked Nauru Island and New Ireland, then worked over the Marshalls and Truk. Just before hitting Kwajalein Atoll, Lt Cdr Vose was transferred to the Bureau of Aeronautics in Washington, DC, where his experience could best be used. He was succeeded by his 'exec,' Lt Cdr Jeff Norman, who took the squadron through the remainder of the cruise, including strikes on Truk and Tinian. When Bombing 17 flew off *Bunker Hill* on 4 March, the Helldiver was still an imperfect instrument, but it was a tested weapon that would be improved for those squadrons yet to fly in VB-17's slipstream.

HELLDIVERS AIR-TO-AIR

SB2C squadrons were credited with 44 confirmed victories in aerial combat and 14 enemy aircraft probably shot down. The top scorer was Lt Robert B Parker of VB-19, who downed three Japanese fighters while flying from *Lexington* in late 1944 – 'Zekie' Parker was killed by the *kamikaze* that struck the ship on 5 November, destroying a gallery on the island where six other VB-19 pilots were killed and five wounded.

Next in line among SB2C pilots was Lt Cdr Arthur L Downing of *Wasp's* Bombing 14, who claimed 1.5 aerial victories. The most successful gunners were ARM3/c E J Elias of the same squadron and ARM3/c S E Wallace of VB-17, each with two confirmed.

Of note is the fact that some air groups transitioned dive-bomber pilots to fighters, often with considerable success. VB-14 aviators claimed eight confirmed and a probable while flying *Wasp's* Hellcats in the summer of 1944, and at least one *Hornet* pilot of VB-2 enjoyed similar success.

Lt 'Red' Carmody, one of the more experienced pilots within VB-8 during the unit's first combat tour with the 'Beast'

Squadron	Ship	Dest	Prob	Dmg	Comments
VB-18	*Intrepid*	12	0	2	
VB-19	*Lexington*	11	1	0	
VB-14	*Wasp*	4.5	0	4	Plus 8 in F6Fs
VB-17	*Bunker Hill*	4	2	3	
VB-2	*Hornet*	3	3	3	Plus 1 in F6Fs
VB-8	*Bunker Hill*	3	3	7	
VB-15	*Essex*	2	1	3.5	
VB-11	*Hornet*	2	0	2	
VB-7	*Hancock*	1	1	0	
VB-80	*Ticonderoga*	1	0	0	
VB-13	*Franklin*	0.5	3	0	
Total		44	14	24.5	

This table gives a detailed breakdown of all SB2C kills, unit by unit. Pilots got the majority of the victories with 24.5 of the total, plus 3.5 others shared with their gunners. The latter claimed 16 by themselves.

One advantage the SB2C enjoyed over the SBD was greater speed, a factor which prompted Lt 'Red' Carmody of VB-8 to attempt an interception of a Mitsubishi G4M 'Betty' near Palau on 31 March 1944;

'In the afternoon I got permission from the CAG to go back with one of my wingmen, who had a hung bomb, to make another bombing run. On the pull-out, low over the water, I spotted a twin-engined bomber coming from the west. It was a "Betty". The pilot turned west and headed low over the water. I told my gunner to close his hatch to decrease the drag and was able to close to 20 mm range and opened fire. After a short burst, the guns jammed, but I kept following the 'Betty', trying to make the guns work. Lucky for me there was no return fire from the tail gunner.

'I was so frustrated that I decided to overtake the 'Betty' and have my gunner shoot at it with his twin .30 cals. When I got up close enough to see the pilot, I told the gunner to open the hatch and shoot it down. As soon as he opened the hatch, however, the "Beast" lost speed and I never could claim a shootdown. If it wasn't for fuel considerations, I would still be after that "Betty"!

'As I recall, I had reached about 210 knots in overtaking the bomber. This wouldn't have been possible in the Dauntless. It was a very disappointing incident, but an exciting 20 minutes of the war, however.'

Three weeks later, during the Hollandia operation, another 'Betty' crossed paths with Helldivers. Lt Harold L Buell was leading nine VB-2 aircraft away from the rendezvous after a close support mission when a G4M was sighted low on the water. As Buell wrly reported, 'Without even considering a call to our fighters in the area, I put the flight into a right echelon and led it down in column on the unsuspecting bogey.'

Perhaps 50 ft off the water, the Mitsubishi had no room to manoeuvre as Buell led a high side attack. His 20 mm shells knocked the cover off the top turret, then each following Helldiver pressed home a gunnery run until the bomber struck the water, exploding on impact. The 'Sea Wolves' had logged their second shootdown, the first having occurred over Peleliu on 30 March.

However, there existed concern as to how a kill should be credited among nine aircraft, all of which had fired on the hapless 'Betty'. Finally it was decided to give official credit to the last three pilots in line, who were still shooting when the bomber splashed!

Helldivers were likely to cross paths with an enormous variety of enemy aircraft. No fewer than 15 Japanese types were represented among the 44 shootdowns, with Zekes, 'Oscars' and 'Bettys' leading the list. However, from late 1944 the opportunity for Helldiver crews to engage enemy aircraft was severely limited, as increasing numbers of carrier fighters perfected their escort technique. The SB2C's last firing encounters with airborne targets probably occurred during the Tokyo strikes of February 1945. Indeed, in the last eight months of the war, only two Navy dive-bombers and five torpedo aircraft were known lost in aerial combat.

Navy monthly summaries indicate that 17 SB2Cs were shot down by Japanese aircraft, the last two being VB-20 Helldivers over Formosa in January 1945. A postwar report states that an additional SB2C was lost in aerial combat, but details are lacking.

Partners in the carrier attack mission were the SB2C Helldiver and Grumman's TBF Avenger. These 'teammates', aboard an unidentified *Essex*-class carrier in 1944, are being manoeuvred into postion by plane handlers, who will 'respot' the deck in preparation for the next launch (*Philip Jarrett*)

A Bombing Two SB2C-1C engages the barrier aboard USS *Hornet* (CV-12) on 24 April 1944. Aircraft number 50 is unusual in that it appears to bear a squadron emblem and mission markers ahead of the pilot's cockpit. The *Hornet* deployment lasted from March to September 1944, and included the Marianas campaign (*Tailhook*)

NIGHTMARE IN THE MARIANAS

The First Battle of the Philippine Sea involved five SB2C squadrons within Task Force 58, with a total of 174 Helldivers. By the time of Operation *Forager* in June 1944, only two fast carriers still retained SBDs – Vice Adm Marc Mitscher's Task Force 58 flagship *Lexington* (CV-16) with VB-16, and her 'team-mate' *Enterprise* (CV-6) with VB-10 *Forager's* goal was twofold – to occupy the main islands of the Marianas (Saipan, Guam and Tinian) and to draw the Japanese Navy into battle, where major fleet units might be destroyed. The following table details the units involved in the battle.

SB2C Squadrons in the Marianas Campaign

VB-1	*Yorktown*	SB2C-1C	Lt Cdr J W Runyan
VB-2	*Hornet*	SB2C-1C	Lt Cdr G B Campbell
VB-8	*Bunker Hill*	SB2C-1	Lt Cdr J D Arbes
VB-14	*Wasp*	SB2C-1C	Lt Cdr J D Blitch
VB-15	*Essex*	SB2C-1C	Lt Cdr J H Mini

The conquest of the Marianas began with a fighter sweep on 11 June, and action continued for most of the following week. Air combat peaked eight days later, when Vice Adm Jisaburo Ozawa's nine carriers arrived west of Saipan and launched a series of attacks against TF-58. On the 19th, Hellcat squadrons claimed more than 350 shootdowns in 'The Great Marianas Turkey Shoot', an action which effectively broke the back of Japanese naval aviation. However, while Ozawa's carriers

Record-setting Air Group 15 broke into combat during strikes on Marcus Island in May 1944. VB-15's lucky number seven returned to *Essex* with half its rudder shredded by a direct hit from enemy flak, but the SB2C-3 survived to fly again (*Jim Sullivan*)

remained unseen by Mitscher's aviators, US submarines found the enemy and torpedoed two of the biggest Japanese 'flattops' remaining afloat – the veteran *Shokaku* and larger, newer, *Taiho*. By sundown the emperor's Mobile Fleet had been reduced from nine flightdecks to seven, and from 439 carrier aircraft to just 70 flyable.

INTO THE DARK

The famous 'mission beyond darkness' of 20 June involved massive losses among SB2C squadrons, with little compensating damage to the enemy. However, there was some room for optimism since nearly all the losses were due to fuel starvation or night-time crashes, rather than the result of enemy action, and the vast majority of pilots and aircrewmen were rescued.

Vice Adm Ozawa had deployed his fleet in three task groups, and retained that organisation even after the loss of two carriers the day before. His 'A Force' (to the north) now contained only *Zuikaku*, while the 'B' and 'C Forces' in the centre and south of his formation were each built around three light carriers.

Despite the long distance – some 300 nautical miles – Mitscher had little doubt in despatching a major strike on the afternoon of the 20th. Japanese carriers had not been engaged since the Battle of Santa Cruz in October 1942 – some 20 months before. For Mitscher, only the 33rd US Navy officer to win his wings, it was too good an opportunity to ignore.

The launch was extremely well executed – TF-58 put up 240 aircraft in barely 12 minutes. Minus 14 'air aborts', the combined strike included 52 SB2Cs, 54 Avengers, 26 Dauntlesses and 95 Hellcats. But the extreme distance to the target was cause for universal concern. Aboard *Hornet*, the air group commander was already convinced that most of his pilots would have to ditch in the sea.

As the first deckload disappeared toward the western horizon, Vice Adm Mitscher cancelled the second launch. Aboard *Bunker Hill*, Lt 'Red' Carmody was turning up prior to leading his 12-aircraft team in a follow-on attack when the 'cut engines' signal came. The Bombing Eight crews returned to their ready

Helldivers and Avengers of Air Group 15 on 27 May 1944 – just prior to the commencement of the Marianas campaign. Trailing CV-9 is the light carrier *San Jacinto* (CVL-30) and *Essex's* sister-ship *Wasp* (CV-18), which had Air Group 14 embarked (*US Navy*)

One of the most dramatic Helldiver photos of the war, this shot captures aircraft of VB-1 overhead USS *Yorktown* (CV-10) in July 1944. Preparing to enter the landing pattern, four of the aircraft already have their tailhooks lowered

A Bombing One aircraft turns into the landing pattern overhead USS *Yorktown* in tight formation with the photo aircraft. VB-1 flew from 'The Fighting Lady' from May to August 1944, participating in the Marianas battle, as well as strikes on the Bonins, Palaus and elsewhere (*Tailhook*)

This SB2C-1C of Bombing Squadron One is seen overhead Task Group 58.1, with an *Essex* class carrier visible in the distance below. During the attack on the Japanese Mobile Fleet on 20 June 1944, VB-1 lost 9 of 14 aircraft despatched, but recovered all 18 downed aircrew (*Tailhook*)

The *Yorktown* task group attacked the Japanese-held Bonin Islands in June and July 1944, sinking shipping and interdicting land-based naval aircraft. Minus the usual tail number, this aircraft carries 250-lb bombs on external wing racks, as well as the standard 1000 'pounder' slung in the bomb bay (*Tailhook*)

room more than a little disappointed at missing a shot at the enemy carriers, but events would prove the wisdom of Mitscher's decision. The latter had decided to retain the second deckload for the morning, as a hedge against unforeseen contingencies.

"GO FOR THE FIGHTING NAVY!"

Like most carriers in the task force, *Wasp* prepared two 'deckload' strikes against the enemy fleet. However, when the second launch was cancelled, the air group commander was left behind. Therefore, leader of Air Group 14's strike was the bomber skipper, Cdr J D Blitch.

The *Wasp* strike comprised 12 SB2C-1Cs, 16 F6F-3 Hellcats and 17 TBF-1C Avengers – 45 aircraft in all. Loadout for the bombers was either a 1000-lb general-purpose or semi armour-piercing bomb, plus two 250 'pounders' under the wings. Each Helldiver carried a full fuel load of 310 gallons.

Trailing *Bunker Hill's* Air Group Eight, Cdr Blitch was drawn south of the search route by radio calls and false radar contacts. Consequently, upon returning to the original track, *Wasp's* aviators felt they had insufficient fuel to pursue what an *Enterprise* squadron commander called 'the fighting navy'. Bombing 14 therefore attacked the Japanese oiler group trailing the three carrier divisions. Blitch, as senior aviator present,

Using radio callsigns 'Jungle 62' and 'Jungle 70,' two VB-1 Helldivers are seen on patrol from *Yorktown* toward the end of their deployment in the summer of 1944
(*US Navy*)

assigned three bombers to each of four oilers and four Avengers to a fifth. He retained a reserve of four TBFs to hit any targets that were missed. Meanwhile, the Hellcats either remained as top cover, bombed oilers with 500 'pounders', or strafed the destroyers to suppress AA fire.

As the air group pulled off target, fliers reported seeing one oiler 'explode and disintegrate', one on fire and one dead in the water, while a fourth was thought to be leaking oil. Recovered pilots and aircrewmen claimed four direct hits and five near misses on four oilers, of which two were confirmed sunk.

Wasp's aviators had in fact inflicted mortal damage on two oilers, as both *Seiyo Maru* and *Genyo Maru* were scuttled, while another ship survived owing to good damage control.

The attack itself was considered successful, but a timing error resulted in a division of F6Fs being out of position when six Mitsubishi A6M5 Zekes attacked. One SB2C was shot down and an F6F also went into the water. However, timely intervention by three unidentified Hellcats prevented further loss among the five bombers, which diverted north of the target, although two VB-14 pilots were wounded. Squadron gunners claimed two Zekes damaged in the running battle in darkening skies.

Bombing Two's second division aircraft, including numbers 49 and 50, climb to altitude after taking off from *Hornet* in June 1944. The squadron attacked *Zuikaku*, the largest surviving Japanese carrier, during the strike of the 20th, inflicting heavy damage
(*Norman Polmar*)

Nearing the task force in total darkness, and not qualified in night landings, the *Wasp* pilots began running out of fuel. Mitscher ordered his ships to turn on their lights, but this courageous, well-intended, gesture led to further problems as few fliers could distinguish a carrier from another ship at night.

Blitch himself later reported;
'The last thing I remember was

Plane handlers move a VB-8 SB2C during operations in June 1944. *Bunker Hill* contributed a dozen Helldivers to the dusk strike on the Japanese fleet off Saipan on the 20th, losing 11 aircraft and 6 pilots or gunners. Most of the losses were attributable to fuel exhaustion or deck crashes (*US Navy*)

VB-8 CO James Arbes led his six-aircraft division against the light carrier *Chiyoda* during the Marianas action. His aircraft was struck several times by flak during his dive from 13,000 ft. Although the Japanese carrier took a direct hit, it survived to fight another day

being about 25 miles from the nearest searchlight. Apparently I passed out and crashed. I came to under water with the cockpit closed. I do not remember getting out of the cockpit, but remember being on the wing and then getting in the rear cockpit to look for my gunner. He was not there and, as the plane sank, I reached for the life raft, which was not in its holder, so I was only able to get out of the plane just as it was sinking.'

Blitch was rescued by a floatplane from the cruiser USS *Canberra* 40 hours later. Only one of his aircraft returned that night, flown by the squadron's junior officer, whose gunner was also the senior radioman. Ens K P Fulton landed aboard *Enterprise* – the first time he had attempted a night carrier landing! It may also have been the first SB2C 'trap' ever logged aboard 'The Big E.'

Thus, *Wasp's* Helldivers sustained 92 per cent losses – one shot down by Zekes and ten ditched out of fuel or crashed in the water. The eight surviving crews reported that their SB2Cs floated for between two-and-a-half to three-and-a-half minutes, even with empty fuel tanks. Those rescued were in the water anywhere from 15 minutes to two days.

The submarine USS *Seawolf*, operating under radio silence after a clandestine reconnaissance of Japanese islands, transited the area of Ozawa's carriers and picked up the last *Wasp* crew to be saved – Lt(jg) A T Walraven and ARM2/c J C Bramer.

OVER THE CARRIERS

The Japanese fleet was divided into three carrier groups and the oiler group. Positioned roughly north to south, the carrier divisions comprised the 'A Force' with *Zuikaku*, the 'B Force' with three light carriers and 'C Force' with three more CVLs.

Focus of most of the SB2Cs was Ozawa's largest remaining carrier, *Zuikaku. Hornet's* VB-2 was probably first to tackle the big ship, a veteran of Pearl Harbor and every carrier engagement but Midway.

Lt Hal Buell flew number 48 on the raid, an SB2C-1C normally assigned to Lt(jg) Dave Steer. Entering his dive at 12,000 ft, Buell immediately encountered heavy flak that made him feel as if he were suspended in space. He therefore closed his dive brakes in order to accelerate out of the worst of the bursting explosions. Then, at roughly 6000 ft, he violated his own

Chief Photographer's mate Johnson is seen with one of the large K-25 cameras issued to each radioman-gunner within VB-8

experience and the SB2C handbook by opening the brakes again. It felt as if 'a giant hand grabbed my plane by the tail'. With a good sight picture, he released at 2000 ft over *Zuikaku*, but more flak and the gathering gloom prevented him from seeing the result.

Buell had more immediate problems. An AA shell exploded in one wing, causing a fire and wounding the young Iowan in the back. Bleeding while flying the damaged aircraft, he set course for Task Force 58 and eventually managed to crash land back aboard *Lexington*.

Following Bombing Two was *Yorktown's* VB-1, led by Lt Cdr J W Runyan. *Yorktown's* air staff had little faith in the reliability of the SB2C-1, and had therefore assigned 15 bombers to a mission order requiring just 12. It proved a wise precaution, for two aircraft had indeed aborted.

Runyan took his squadron over the big carrier and dived from 15,000 ft. Bombing One reported heavy and accurate AA fire which jostled the aircraft both in their dives and while retiring to the rendezvous. Releases were typically made below 2000 ft, with claims for three direct hits and numerous near misses. In the gathering darkness and heavy flak, *Zuikaku* was seen to be afire, so Runyan's last two pilots diverted and dropped their bombs on an escorting cruiser instead.

War correspondent W Eugene Smith was a favourite aboard *Bunker Hill*, and he accompanied VB-8 on many memorable actions during its war cruise of 1944

Zuikaku survived the attentions of VB-1 and -2, plus six *Hornet* Avengers. Two-dozen heavy bombs had been aimed at her, and an unknown number struck home to start fires on the hangar deck. The Japanese action report lists one direct hit and six or more near misses, which seems conservative, because at one point the word was passed to abandon ship. However, fire-fighters got the blazes under control and the 28,000-ton carrier survived.

Three air group formations tackled 'C Force' to the south, including the *Bunker Hill* contingent. Lt Cdr J D Arbes' VB-8 went after light carrier *Chiyoda* with his six-aircraft division from the south-east, while Lt A D Jones' division attacked from the north. With four battleships in attendance, 'C Force' was well protected, and Arbes felt several flak hits on his bomber during his dive from 13,000 ft. At one point he glanced out to see holes in the top of his wing, but he pressed home the attack and dropped at about 2000 ft. By the time Jones' division attacked, the light carrier was

still manoeuvring, but seemed to be emitting smoke. Arbes' pilots claimed six hits on the carrier and three more on two escorts.

According to Japanese sources, *Chiyoda* took one hit aft on the flight-deck, resulting in only slight damage. Whatever her wounds, she steamed away without difficulty. However, *Hiyo* succumbed to torpedo damage from *Bunker Hill's* Avengers, becoming the third carrier lost in 48 hours.

Five *Bunker Hill* SB2Cs which had raced past the Japanese destroyer screen at low level were expertly attacked from six o'clock low. Five or more Zekes closed to within gun range undetected, and downed two Helldivers – one crashed into the water and the other went in burning. The three remaining 'Beasts' survived damage from 7.7 and 20 mm fire.

With the 20-minute attack now completed, Mitscher's aviators faced a two-hour return to Task Force 58 through inky tropical darkness. The table on the next page lists the losses suffered by the Helldiver units.

Bunker Hill plane handlers lean into a 30-mph breeze as they escort a VB-8 Helldiver up the deck. Typical air plans called for at least two full deckload strikes during sustained operations, plus numerous auxiliary missions such as anti-submarine patrol, all of which placed a premium on fast, efficient 'reshuffling the deck' (*Phil Jarrett*)

Yet another barrier engagement resulted in this VB-15 aircraft being written off during support of the Saipan landings. Crewmen are spraying aqueous foam – a fire retarden – into the ruptured airframe as a precaution against the ignition of volatile high-octane aviation fuel (*Jim Sullivan*)

Squadron	ship	SB2C Sortied	SB2Cs Lost	Pilots Lost	Aircrew Lost
VB-1	Yorktown	14	9	0	0
VB-2	Hornet	14	12	1	2
VB-8	Bunker Hill	12	11	3	3
VB-14	Wasp	12	11	4	5

Of 52 SB2Cs despatched, only 8 returned safely (only 2 VB-1 pilots found their carrier) for an 85 per cent loss rate. Thirty-five SB2Cs/SBWs ditched out of fuel, with four crews and one gunner not recovered. Four were lost in combat in the vicinity of the Japanese ships, while four more crashed attempting to land back aboard TF-58's carriers. Aircrew losses totalled eight pilots and ten radioman-gunners.

During the month of June, the five SB2C units in TF-58 lost 81 aircraft to all causes, led by *Hornet's* Bombing Two with 22. *Yorktown's* VB-1 struck off 19, *Bunker Hill's* VB-8 17, while *Wasp's* unfortunate VB-14 lost 13 and *Essex's* VB-15, which was spared the 'mission beyond darkness,' lost 10. With operational casualties in other areas, June 1944 was the second-worst month for Helldiver losses in the war – a total of 97. But such was the price of waging global conflict.

Japanese anti-aircraft fire clipped the starboard stabiliser of this VB-15 Helldiver, which nevertheless made it safely back aboard *Essex*. The squadron lost 10 SB2Cs to all causes during the month of June – the lowest toll of any frontline Helldiver unit in the Pacific at that time. This was due primarily to the fact that *Essex's* strike was held as a reserve following the launch against the enemy carriers on the 20th (*Jim Sullivan*)

Hornet ordnancemen push two Mk 13 torpedoes toward VB-2 Helldivers during the summer of 1944. Although SB2Cs were capable of carrying aerial torpedoes when bomb bay doors were removed and special shackles installed, apparently the scheme was never employed operationally. This evolution may have been a loading drill intended to keep the option viable (*US Navy*)

DECISION AT LEYTE

merica's return to the Philippine Islands in the autumn of 1944 precipitated one of the greatest naval battles of all time. Occasionally called the 'Second Philippine Sea', it is better known as the sprawling three-day Battle of Leyte Gulf.

By September, when preliminary strikes began, Helldivers equipped all eight fast carrier bombing squadrons. Two were veterans of the Marianas – VB-14 in *Wasp* and VB-15 in *Essex*. One of the others, Bombing 11, which replaced VB-2 in *Hornet*, retained some experienced aircrew from the 1943 tour at Guadalcanal.

Among the least distinctive markings seen on carrier-based Helldivers were the plain white numbers painted on the tails of VB-13 aircraft aboard USS *Franklin* (CV-13). Dated July 1944, this photo was taken at the beginning of the squadron's four-month combat tour aboard 'Big Ben', VB-13 having been mated with the new carrier since the previous March (*Tailhook*)

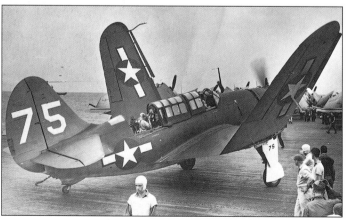

Winning the prize for the most distinctive unit markings was VB-19, which painted enormous white numbers on the tails of its SB2C-3s. Relieving VB-16 aboard *Lexington* in July 1944, Bombing 19 was the first Helldiver squadron to fly from Vice Adm M A Mitscher's flagship. Air Group 19 was unusual in that each of its squadrons had a different 'G' symbol rather than the same emblem for all. Fighting 19's Hellcats had numbers painted behind the cockpit while Torpedo 19 used an inverted triangle (*Tailhook*)

Also, by this time the 'dash three' Helldiver had replaced the SB2C-1s and -1Cs, the new variant being universally regarded as a far superior aircraft to the original model, although not without some reluctance at task force level. Vice Adm Mitscher, who had been impressed with the performance of the SBD-equipped VB-10 and -16 off Saipan, had actually considered retroactively placing Dauntlesses back in his bombing squadrons. However, Douglas Aircraft ceased production of the Dauntless in July, leaving him no alternative but to continue absorbing -2Cs.

SB2C Squadrons in the Battle of Leyte Gulf

VB-7	*Hancock*	SB2C-3/3E	Lt Cdr J L Erickson
VB-11	*Hornet*	SB2C-3	Lt Cdr L A Smith
VB-13	*Franklin*	SB2C-3	Lt C A Skinner
VB-14	*Wasp*	SB2C-3	Lt Cdr J D Blitch
VB-15	*Essex*	SB2C-3	Lt Cdr J H Mini
VB-18	*Intrepid*	SB2C-3	Lt Cdr M Eslick
VB-19	*Lexington*	SB2C-3	Lt Cdr R McGowan
VB-20	*Enterprise*	SB2C-3	Cdr R E Riera

Now retired Vice Adm Donald Engen was then a 19-year-old ensign in VB-19, which relieved VB-16 aboard Mitscher's flagship *Lexington* in July 1944. The squadron had hastily converted from SBDs to Helldivers, with some lingering doubts;

'The SB2C-1 was a dog of an aeroplane and deserved the name "Beast". This term really came from the fact there were a lot of sharp edges (dive brakes and bomb bay doors), and those who worked on them kept getting "bit" by them and bled a lot.

'When we joined *Lexington*, it was clear that Vice Adm Mitscher had a low opinion of the SB2C. It was big, difficult to move around on deck, hard to fit into corners, took more maintenance, and in his view had not acquitted itself well in combat. He was feeling the loss of the aeroplanes in the Philippine Sea battle. At first he just tolerated us. But the SB2C-3 was an entirely different aeroplane than the -1s/-1Cs that we had flown earlier. The bigger engine, and the electric-governed four-bladed propeller, gave it much more power. The nightmarish hydraulic system with its four separate garden-faucet style valves on the cockpit floor was improved. It still "weeped" a little hydraulic

The first division of VB-19 was composed of the CO, Lt Cdr R S McGowan, and his two wingmen in the lead section, plus three more pilots in the second section. Seen in this group shot are, at the rear from left to right, L A Hielman, R S McGowan and Jack Scott, whilst in the front from left to right, W P Wodell, E E Newman and H N Walters (*Cdr William Emerson*)

fluid here and there, but it was actually a pleasant aeroplane to fly and honest in the aerodynamic sense. Of course, we had our maintenance challenges, but on balance the aeroplane and VB-19 turned Mitscher's low opinion around in about 60 days. He became a supporter, and even sent word down to Ready Room Two in early September that he had changed his mind. From then on the aeroplane was on his team.'

Another source of admiration for the Helldiver was its ability to survive battle damage. During early operations against the Philippines, the pilots of VB-8 learned that it took more than a heavy line to 'hogtie' a 'Beast'. Martin Carmody recalled;

'Following one of our strikes on Cebu, I took the flight north to Legaspi Harbour, on southern Luzon, looking for ships. As we approached the harbour I could see a merchant-type vessel alongside a pier, and directed the flight to follow me for a steep angle of attack with our 20 mms. I could see that my bullets were hitting amidship, and as I pulled up turning, I could see that one of my wingmen was also on target and the second wing-man was just pulling up when he caught the full blast of the ship's cargo of ammunition exploding. I felt that my wingman, Carl Mayer, was lost

for sure. After a short period of time, I received a radio call from Carl stating that he was at 5000 ft and all battered up and would have to bail out. I told him to keep flying east to the open ocean and keep airborne as long as he could, and we would join him.

'When we rendezvoused, I could see that the aircraft's underside was badly bashed in, and there were holes everywhere. The bottom half of the engine cowl was gone and oil was leaking on the exhaust pipe, causing a stream of smoke behind the aircraft. Additionally, about 60 ft of the ship's mooring hauser was

Briefing for VB-19's first combat launch from USS *Lexington* 18 July 1944. The subject of this 0630 brief was an Air Group 19 attack on Guam. First row, from left to right, J B Gunter and D D Engen. Second row, W S Emerson, W Koch and A F Emig. Third row, R G Wicklander, W T Good and J W Evatt. Fourth row, E D Stella and W E McBride. Standing, P A Gevelinger. Donald Engen, then a 19-year-old ensign, retired as a vice admiral and later became director of the National Air and Space Museum in Washington, DC (*Cdr William Emerson*)

caught around the leading edge of the right wing, making it difficult to use the right aileron. I attempted to loosen the hauser with my left wing a couple of times without success. The weight of the longer piece gradually caused the hauser to slide off the wing. With the engine still running well, Carl opted not to land alongside a rescue submarine but continue on to the carrier. Neither he or his crewman were injured, and he made the recovery without incident. The flight deck officer took one look at the aircraft and ordered it to be pushed over the side.'

SIBUYAN SEA AND CAPE ENGANO

On 24 October the fast carriers launched a series of air strikes against major Japanese fleet units in the Sibuyan Sea, west of the Philippines. The Imperial Navy deployed in a three-pronged effort to penetrate to Leyte Gulf, where the US Seventh Fleet lay vulnerable with its amphibious shipping and light covering forces. Toward that end, a deception force involving four carriers steamed off the north-east coast of Leyte, while two powerful surface units arrived from the west – one intending to transit San Bernardino Strait and the other to head south via Surigao Strait, between Luzon and Mindanao. The latter force was destroyed by surface action on the night of 24 October; whilst the centre force was attacked repeatedly that day.

Taken roughly eight hours after the previous photo, this view shows preparations for VB-19's fourth mission to Guam on 18 July 1944. Front row, P A Gevelinger, R G Wicklander and D D Engen. Second row, E D Stella, R F Majors and A F Emig. Third row, G Glumac, W S Emerson, D F Banker and W E McBride. The two pilots at the rear of the ready room were not assigned to this flight (*Cdr William Emerson*)

Operating by task groups, Mitscher's aviators launched six strikes throughout the day. Overflying the Philippines from east to west, they reached the centre force in the Sibuyan Sea between Palawan and the Philippines. The first strike to arrive was from Task Group 38.2, which included Air Group 18 from *Intrepid* (CV-11). The bombing squadron had taken heavy losses – its original skipper in training,

Bombing Squadron 14 joined USS *Wasp* (CV-18) with the ship's original air group in January 1944, and remained aboard for most of the year. Combat highlights were the Philippine Sea and Leyte Gulf battles during perhaps the longest time any SB2C squadron spent aboard one carrier. Operations against the Palau Islands in August resulted in this 'Beast' colliding with one of the ship's aft 5-in anti-aircraft turrets (*Tailhook*)

VB-7's G symbol whilst aboard USS *Hancock* (CV-19) was the sketched Greek letter Omega, as is clearly visible in this shot of a squadron SB2C-3 in October 1944. This Helldiver has its own personal escort in the form of a glossy sea blue Hellcat from VF-7, also part of Air Group 7

and then during strikes against Formosa, several senior lieutenants and the next commanding officer, Lt Cdr Mark Eslick, had all been killed in action. During the first three weeks of October a dozen aircraft had been lost, mainly to operational causes. However, the squadron benefited from the presence of some highly experienced scout-bomber pilots like Lts Benjamin G Preston and Leif Larsen, who had flown SBDs from the original *Yorktown* (CV-5) at Coral Sea and Midway.

Now under Lt Cdr George Ghesquiere, Bombing 18 launched 12 Helldivers against the Centre Force in company with 10 Avenger torpedo bombers and 4 Hellcat fighters. The paucity of F6Fs testified to just how thinly stretched the fast carriers were at this point – on 24 October, which was one of the three heaviest days of aerial combat in the Pacific War, the task force was hard pressed to meet requirements for combat air patrols and strike escort.

Cruising at 17,000 ft, the *Intrepid* formation of just 26 aircraft sighted Vice Adm Takeo Kurita's armada of 29 warships. However, help was at hand – other air groups were assigned targets as CVG-18 neared the formation, and the Japanese lacked air cover. The pilots could concentrate on bombing without fear of interception.

At 1025 Lt Cdr Ghesquiere set up his attack on one of two huge battleships, which proved to be the 64,000-ton *Musashi*, mounting 18-in guns. In a sudden wingover, the lead Helldiver dropped vertically on the juggernaut, plunging through brown-black explosions of heavy AA shells and a criss-cross pattern of vari-coloured tracers.

Some pilots took evasive action in their dives, hoping to compound the enemy gunners' tracking, but there was no evading barrage fire – aviators could only dive through the flak-studded sky. Finally, at around 6000 ft, they steadied up, ignoring the nearby sound of exploding shells and the high-pitched whine of shrapnel penetrating their Helldivers' aluminum skins. Most of VB-18 released at around 2000 ft, with *Musashi* looking huge and grey through the bombsight. Then the vivid picture was lost in the grey-black fog of a 10-G pullout.

Heavy bombs rippled across *Musashi's* armoured deck and turrets, while Avengers punched torpedoes into her hull. The process continued for hours, with air groups from each task group alternately arriving on scene. The second strike, similar in composition to the first, went in at 1245. Progress was slow

Another 'plankowner' SB2C squadron, VB-7 was part of *Hancock's* first air group. Between September 1944 and January 1945 Bombing Seven participated in the Philippines campaign and strikes against Formosa, among other operations. This photo of an SB2C-3 shows a variety of unusual features, including the twin .30-cal gun pod fitted beneath the dive-bomber's wing, the squadron's distinctive narrow white band around the cowling and the individual aircraft name 'Satan's Angel' below the cockpit (*Tailhook*)

but steady – when the third attack rolled in at 1330, *Musashi* was clearly stricken. *Lexington* and *Essex* aviators from TG-38.3 found the dreadnought trailing the main force by some 20 miles.

Enterprise's Air Group 20 from TG-38.4 arrived with 16 Hellcats, 14 Helldivers and 8 Avengers at 1415, nearly six hours after the first wave. They were met with a spectacular display of Japanese pyrotechnics as shells exploded three miles high in shades of purple, red, yellow, blue and white. The on-scene air co-ordinator assigned 'The Big E's' bombers and torpedo aircraft to *Musashi*, while VF-20 attacked a cruiser to suppress AA fire. The plan worked, as when the *Enterprise* airmen pulled away the huge battleship was down by the bow, having been hit by as many as eight torpedoes and ten or more bombs.

Typical of these missions was a 5.5-hour flight by VB-19 from *Lexington*. However, Bombing 19's skipper, Cdr Richard McGowan of the Annapolis class of 1935, was forced to abort with electrical problems. After waiting near the task force while a Japanese raid was repulsed, another of McGowan's pilots landed ahead of him. Making a long, flat approach to *Lexington*, McGowan's Helldiver abruptly crashed close astern. His wingman, Lt Jack Scott, flew past to drop a smoke flare to mark the spot, but-tragically McGowan was lost in the ditching, although his gunner, E A Brown, was saved. Another loss on the 24th was the bomber flown by Lt E E Newman, shot down by a Japanese fighter just beyond the task force screen. One of the destroyers picked him up.

Lexington's 'team-mate' almost lost her bomber skipper as Cdr J H Mini ditched near *Essex* upon

The Japanese light carrier *Zuiho* is seen under attack by Task Force 38 aircraft on 25 October 1944. Despite her dazzle-painted flightdeck resembling a battleship or cruiser, the carrier has taken bomb hits along her centreline, and is gushing smoke from her starboard beam. She was sunk along with *Zuikaku*, *Chiyoda* and *Chitose* on this date, which was the last time that Japanese carriers were attacked in the open sea (*Tillman*)

USS *Intrepid's* (CV-11) distinctive air group emblem was a simple 'plus' sign on the tail. This SB2C-3 has returned to 'Evil I' with battle damage visible on the rudder, having just participated in a strike against the Japanese battleship force in the Sibuyan Sea on 25 October 1944 at the height of the Battle for Leyte Gulf (*Tailhook*)

Typical of the SB2C's secondary missions was the anti-submarine patrol. This VB-18 aircraft enters *Intrepid's* landing pattern after an uneventful search, still bearing two 350-lb depth charges beneath its wings (*Phil Jarrett*)

returning from the first *Musashi* strike. His ten Helldivers claimed hits on three battleships, including both *Musashi* and *Yamato*, while the second deckload strike concentrated on the former vessel but lost an SB2C and crew in the process. Lt(jg) C W Crellin had just dropped his bomb, which struck the target, when his aircraft sustained a direct hit by heavy-calibre flak. Crellin and Radioman E E Shetler were killed in action, having contributed to sinking one of the world's largest warships. Total SB2C losses on the 24th amounted to ten aeroplanes, including seven to anti-aircraft guns. The major portion of these were incurred in strikes against the *Musashi/Yamato* force, five of which belonged to *Intrepid's* Bombing 18.

Owing to the nature of their respective weapons, TBF/TBM Avengers probably inflicted more damage on Japanese ships than dive-bombers and fighters armed with bombs and rockets. However, torpedo squadrons sustained losses similar to SB2Cs, with 11 Avengers reported lost to all causes.

Mitscher's sixth, and last, wave attacked at 1842 that evening, more than eight hours after the initial strike. *Musashi* finally succumbed about 50 minutes later, the victim of one of the most sustained air attacks ever launched against ships at sea. Additionally, *Yamato* and *Nagato* sustained at least two bomb hits each while the veteran *Haruna* reported five near-misses.

Although *Musashi* and a cruiser were sunk by carrier aircraft on the 24th, Vice Adm Kurita was not long deterred. After briefly reversing course and reorganising, he turned eastward again that evening and continued through San Bernardino Strait. When his formidable battleship-cruiser force emerged into Leyte Gulf on the morning of the 25th, only a small escort carrier group stood between him and the thin-skinned transports supporting Gen Douglas MacArthur's troops ashore. The ensuing Battle off Samar was fought by Avengers, Wildcats and destroyers or destroyer escorts.

FOUR 'FLATTOPS' SUNK

The next day, 25 October, VB-19's Lt(jg) Stuart E Crapser was assigned a sector search east of due north from Task Force 38 – an outbound leg of 300 nautical miles. His gunner was ARM1/c James F Burns.

Flying at about 1000 ft, Crapser was 20 minutes into his return leg when Burns got radar contact at seven miles, ahead and to port. First

one ship, then several more, came into view. Flying closer, Burns realized that the 'barges' he originally saw were in fact Japanese aircraft carriers;

'I started to climb into a circle outside of AA range, and composed a contact message. Burns copied the text and sent it out three times over the medium high frequency radio and twice over VHF. At this point I decided it was too late for Vice Adm Marc Mitscher to send out a strike and recover it before dark, so I should use (my 1000-lb) bomb to damage one of the carriers. I dropped the empty wing tanks and climbed to 14,000 ft, during which time some AA shells were sent in our

direction. When this happened, Burns threw out some of the aluminum strips called "window", which were supposed to confuse gunfire radar. I observed one carrier head into the wind and launch some aircraft.

'By this time I was positioned for a dive out of the sun. I pushed over at a 60° angle and dived without flaps. My helmet fell off in the dive – I had not fastened the chin strap. I "pickled off" the bomb and felt the aircraft knocked into a spin to the right. I contemplated leaving the aircraft but was able to stop the spin, pull out, and head for some clouds below. The anti-aircraft fire was heavy and I saw tracer pass us from above. I reached the clouds, levelled off in them, and flew for some time southward in and out of them. I noted that the upper surface of the wings was wrinkled and both ailerons were pointing up!'

Burns reported that the Helldiver was shot up, that some Zekes had made runs on them, that he had a slight nick over one eye, that there were two *Shokaku* carriers, one CVL and one light cruiser in the group of ships that he had dived on, and that he had shot down one Zeke. They were not pursued once they had flown into the clouds.

In the heat of the moment, the ship recognition was surprisingly good. Ozawa's force included IJNS *Zuikaku* (sister of *Shokaku*, sunk off Saipan) and three light carriers. Upon returning to *Lexington*, Crapser skillfully got his damaged bomber down safely and reported his finding to Vice Adm Mitscher. The pilot then learned that an anti-aircraft shell had exploded in the port wing – the cause of the spin – and that his bomb had never released!

Two other VB-19 crews also

Helldivers bomb the cruiser *Nachi* in Manila Bay on 5 November 1944. The 13,000-ton vessel sustained direct hits from *Ticonderoga* SB2Cs before *Lexington's* Air Group 19 finished the job off with bombs and torpedoes – at the cost of Lt Donald Banker, the new CO of VB-19. Later, US divers recovered a treasure trove from *Nachi*, which was carrying vital documents relating to the defence of Japan as well as 2,000,000 yen ($500,000) in currency (*Tillman*)

Bombing Four was in continual combat from *Bunker Hill* between 1 and 19 November 1944, participating in Philippines and Formosa strikes. The unit flew the same SB2C-3s as its predecessor, VB-8, during this period (*Jim Sullivan*)

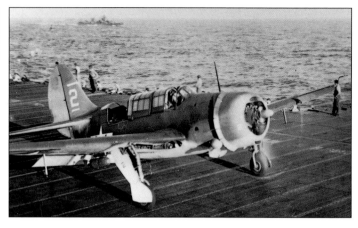

A VB-4 Helldiver prepares for a deck-run take-off from *Bunker Hill* on 13 November 1944. Targets struck on this date included Japanese naval and air bases on Luzon, in the Philippine Islands (*Jim Sullivan*)

Transferred minus aircraft from *Bunker Hill*, VB-4 succeeded VB-15 aboard *Essex* in late November 1944, but retained CV-9's markings and many of its me SB2Cs. Following this mission, medical corpsmen were fortunately unoccupied following the recovery, as they return with an empty woven-wire litter to the lower right of the photo. VB-4 remained in *Essex* until 9 March 1945 (*Jim Sullivan*)

found elements of Vice Adm Ozawa's force off Cape Engano. Thus, *Lexington's* bombers played a major role in Adm W F Halsey's decision to take the fast carriers north, away from Leyte Gulf, in the last air attack ever mounted against carriers operating in the open sea.

Most SB2C squadrons flew two or more strikes against Japan's last operational carriers. CAG-19, Cdr Hugh Winters (see Osprey *Aircraft of the Aces 10 - Hellcat Aces of World War 2* by Barrett Tillman) directed his own air group and many others in a series of attacks that put all four of Ozawa's 'flattops' on the bottom. A contingency strike was launched that morning with orders to circle north of the task force until a definite contact report arrived. The carrier aircraft had only completed one orbit when word came of Ozawa's force 100 miles north.

First to attack was *Essex's* Air Group 15, followed by *Lexington's* Air Group 19. The dozen Helldivers of VB-15's first strike were directed against a light carrier – probably *Chitose* – which was burning as the bombers pulled off the target. The squadron CO, Cdr Mini, was still aboard a destroyer after ditching the day before, so *Essex's* Helldivers were led by Lts J D Bridgers and R F Noyes.

On the second attack, airborne observers credited Bombing 15 with 50 per cent hits on *Zuikaku*, and Bombing 19 with perhaps 12 out of 18. A VT-19 pilot circling nearby watched 'Lex's' last three Helldivers attack, and observed three hits by Lt Jack Meeker and his two wingmen. Thus ended the career of 'Happy Crane', Japan's 'fightingest flattop'.

Strikes continued throughout the day, as many pilots flew two or even three sorties. On the last two missions no carriers remained, so units and divisions were directed against battleships and cruisers instead. VB-19 pilot W S Emerson confided to his diary, 'I saw the most concentrated AA fire I have ever seen, or hope to see. It was a day I'll never forget as long as I live, and I really mean it when I say, "History was made today!"'

Helldiver squadrons certainly accounted for a significant share in the destruction of Ozawa's carriers on the 25th. Compared to the previous day's activities in the Sibuyan Sea, the battle off Cape Engano was even more satisfactory in that only six dive-bombers were lost, including one operationally. Heaviest hit was *Franklin's* VB-13 which lost two crews killed in action.

Meanwhile, Task Group 38.1 struck the surface force of Vice Adm Takeo Kurita, which was threatening US amphibious shipping in Leyte Gulf. Thirteen Helldivers

were lost to all causes in this portion of the action, including seven of *Hancock's* Bombing Seven.

In all, this climactic day of the Philippines campaign involved the loss of 19 Helldivers. However, only eight of these were directly attributable to enemy action, and a further three were jettisoned with heavy damage, while five or more were non-combat losses.

Some squadrons had suffered punishing casualties during sustained operations in October. VB-18, for instance, wrote off 25 Helldivers during missions against Formosa and the Philippines – three to enemy aircraft, six to flak and two jettisoned with heavy damage. The remaining 14 were lost to a variety of operational causes – not an unusual proportion for late-war bombing squadrons.

The last significant shipping attack of the campaign occurred during strikes against Manila Harbour on 5 November. *Ticonderoga's* VB-80 and the tireless VB-19 shared the destruction of the 13,000-ton heavy cruiser *Nachi*, with a notable assist from Torpedo 19. Adm Shima's flagship went down by the stern, broke in three pieces, and sank – a major success, but for the loss of Lt Don Banker, VB-19's second CO in only 11 days.

However, *kamikaze* pilots also enjoyed success that day, as a well-flown Zeke smashed itself against *Lexington's* island. Among the 47 men killed were six VB-19 pilots, plus three more badly injured. The damage resulted in Air Group 19's combat deployment ending prematurely.

Still using the familiar 'Hornet ball' originated by Air Group Two, this VB-11 Helldiver prepares to land aboard CV-12 in late 1944. Between October 1944 and January 1945 Bombing 11 attacked targets in the Philippines, on Formos and Okinawa and in French Indochina. In that period the squadron lost 17 aircraft to all causes, including one to Japanese fighters and at least four to anti-aircraft fire (*Tailhook*)

POST-LEYTE OPERATIONS

The pace of operations hardly eased after the Battle of Leyte Gulf. Fast carrier task groups remained in combat throughout November, resulting in nearly 50 more Helldivers lost in Philippine operations that month, although fewer than 20 were directly attributable to enemy action.

Back aboard *Franklin* (CV-13), a VB-13 pilot examines flak damage to his aircraft while his gunner handles both their parachutes on the starboard wing. The squadron flew from 'Big Ben' between July and October 1944 (*Peter Mersky*)

One of the heaviest losses sustained by any SB2C squadron in this period occurred during an *Essex* strike on Japanese shipping on 11 November. Cdr J H Mini, leading VB-15, attacked a convoy approaching Ormoc Bay, on the island of Leyte, that morning. Composed of six transports and five destroyers, the convoy was capable of a stout defence. While F6Fs bombed and strafed, Mini's lead division quickly sank a transport – the second division Helldivers then scored multiple hits on two more.

However, three SB2Cs were shot down during the attack and another splashed with severe damage, the

crew being rescued by friendly Filipinos. Another Helldiver succumbed to flak damage near the task force, but the pilot and gunner were picked up by a screening destroyer. Meanwhile, in a rare occurrence Lt J W Barnitz diverted to the US Army airfield at Tacloban, where his wounded gunner, Radioman H N Stiekemeyter, received emergency medical treatment.

It was a hard day for Bombing 15 – three crews killed, one temporarily missing and five aircraft lost in flight, plus another jettisoned. Aircrew morale suffered temporarily, but Air Group 15's combat deployment ended with a final attack on Manila Bay three days later. However, an additional loss was incurred on that last mission when Lt(jg) R L Turner and Radioman S Dorosh were killed by anti-aircraft fire. Theirs was the tenth Helldiver that the squadron had lost that month, and the 33rd since VB-15 had entered combat six months before.

The single greatest cause of SB2C attrition during December occurred

A VB-20 SB2C-3 is attended by *Enterprise* (CV-6) flightdeck personnel and medical corpsmen following the Yap strike of 24 November 1944. The gunner is being lifted from his cockpit with wounds sustained in the operation in the Caroline Islands. Aboard 'The Big E' since August, Air Group 20 moved to *Lexington* on 23 November, where it remained until late January 1945 (*Tailhook*)

This VB-7 aircraft withdraws from an attack on Axis shipping along the Indochina coast on 12 January 1945. This operation was the first time Allied ships had entered the South China Sea in nearly three years, seeking Japanese battleships reported to be in the area. In truth, the only warship sunk was a disarmed Vichy French cruiser (*Tailhook*)

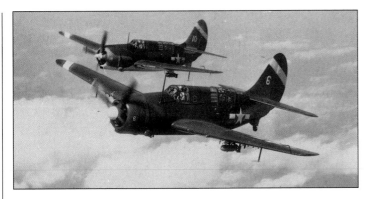

A pair of Bombing 80 Helldivers with underwing ordnance are seen in late 1944. Air Group 80 originally deployed aboard USS *Ticonderoga* (CV-14) in August 1944, and launched its first combat missions against Luzon in November. Following *kamikaze* damage in January 1945, the air group transferred to *Hancock* (CV-19) until returning to the United States in April (*Tailhook*)

With its 'leaping panther' badge below the windscreen, this Bombing Squadron Three SB2C-3 flew from *Yorktown* (CV-10) between November 1944 and March 1945. VB-3 was perhaps the premier Navy attack squadron of World War 2, having been established in 1934 and sinking Japanese warships at Midway and Guadalcanal while flying SBDs. Re-equipped with SB2Cs, the 'Panthers' logged combat against the Japanese in the Philippines, on Formosa and in the home islands (*Tailhook*)

on the 18th when a monstrous typhoon hammered the task force with gale-force winds. At least 24 SB2C-3s were written off whilst aboard the replenishment escort carriers *Altamaha* (CVE-18) and *Cape Esperance* (CVE-88). As many more were lost in routine operations throughout the Navy, with none accountable to combat.

As flight (operations) officer of Bombing 11, Lt Ed Wilson led every third strike for *Hornet's* bombers. He flew with Radioman Harry Jespersen, who had been his rear seat man during VB-11's land-based tour at Guadalcanal in 1943, so the pair were an unusually experienced team. Wilson recalls one of their more harrowing missions together;

'Harry Jespersen had much to do as my eyes to the rear, viewing the radar, helping on rendezvous and firing his guns while monitoring the radio. I gave him the additional duty of looking for secondary targets. After bombing the primary target, I would strafe with my 20 mm cannon and Jespersen with his guns shot up trucks, planes, boats, hangars, etc. He was outstanding in spotting and firing on these targets.

'On 5 November 1944 I led an attack on Clark Field, Luzon. After dropping my bomb I went low to strafe planes on the field. On returning to *Hornet* for landing I got a wave-off for no tailhook. Jespersen crawled back into the tail but was unable to force the tailhook down. So we were brought aboard, going up on our nose when we hit the barrier. Small-arms fire had struck our tailhook.

'On 16 January 1945 I led an attack on the Kowloon docks in Hong Kong Harbour. If it had not been for Jespersen's fast thinking, it would have been our last flight. When I dropped my bomb and pulled out, our plane started flipping around, out of control. I told Jespersen to bail out and he said, "Mr Wilson, lower the wheels", which I did immediately. The plane stabilised, just, over the water, and I flew between Japanese destroyers that were firing up at the diving planes. What happened was that one wheel came down when I pulled a lot of Gs on pulling out, and with all that drag on one side, it was an unstable plane. Jespersen, with his fast thinking, saved my life, his life, and a Navy aircraft. We were too low for a parachute to open if we did bail out. With wheels down we flew back to *Hornet*.

'Harry Jespersen's service in World War 2 earned him a Distinguished Flying Cross, eight Air Medals and a Purple Heart.'

The close teamwork of Ed Wilson and Harry Jespersen was at the heart of the success achieved by every Helldiver unit aboard every carrier committed to combat during World War 2.

COLOUR PLATES

This 10-page section profiles more SB2C Helldivers in colour than has ever been previously seen in one single volume. The colour artwork has been specially-commissioned for this volume, and profile artist Tom Tullis and figure artist Mike Chappell have gone to great pains to illustrate the aircraft, and their crews, as accurately as possible following in-depth research from original sources.

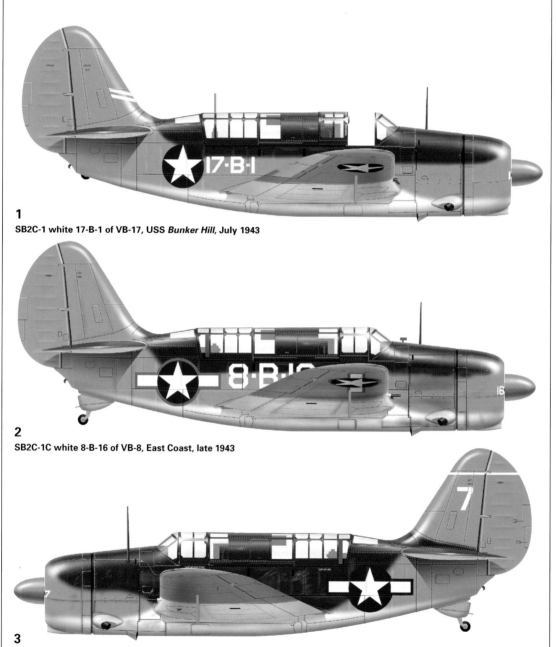

1
SB2C-1 white 17-B-1 of VB-17, USS *Bunker Hill*, July 1943

2
SB2C-1C white 8-B-16 of VB-8, East Coast, late 1943

3
SB2C-3 white 7 of VB-15, USS *Essex*, 20 May 1944

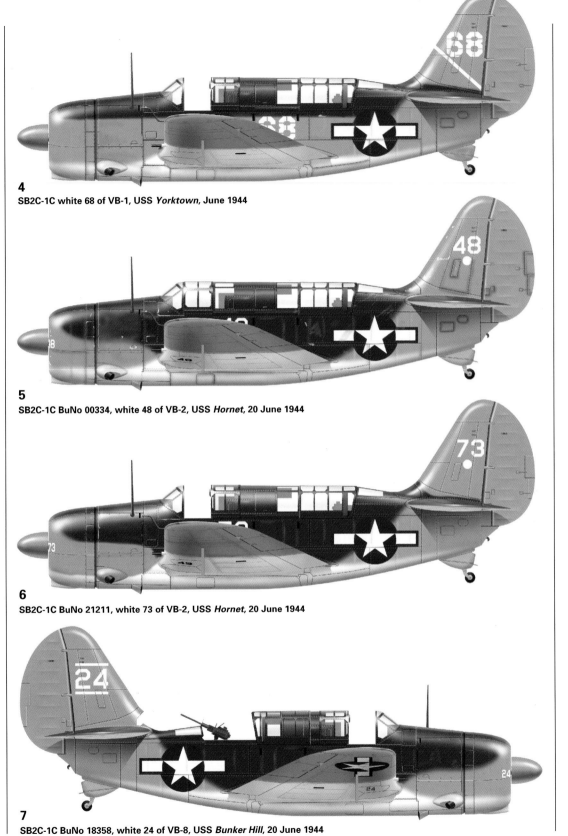

4
SB2C-1C white 68 of VB-1, USS *Yorktown*, June 1944

5
SB2C-1C BuNo 00334, white 48 of VB-2, USS *Hornet*, 20 June 1944

6
SB2C-1C BuNo 21211, white 73 of VB-2, USS *Hornet*, 20 June 1944

7
SB2C-1C BuNo 18358, white 24 of VB-8, USS *Bunker Hill*, 20 June 1944

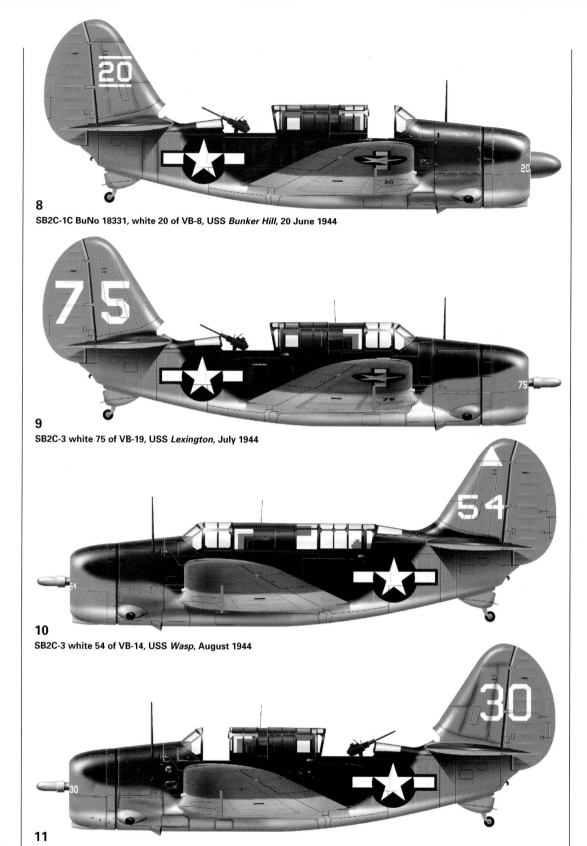

8
SB2C-1C BuNo 18331, white 20 of VB-8, USS *Bunker Hill*, 20 June 1944

9
SB2C-3 white 75 of VB-19, USS *Lexington*, July 1944

10
SB2C-3 white 54 of VB-14, USS *Wasp*, August 1944

11
SB2C-3 white 30 of VB-13, USS *Franklin*, 7 August 1944

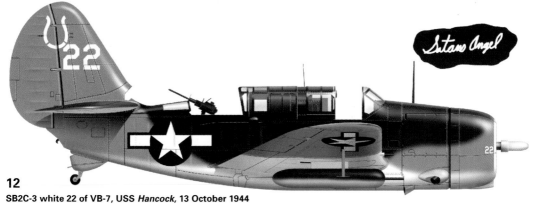

12
SB2C-3 white 22 of VB-7, USS *Hancock*, 13 October 1944

13
SB2C-3 white 61 of VB-18, USS *Intrepid*, 25 October 1944

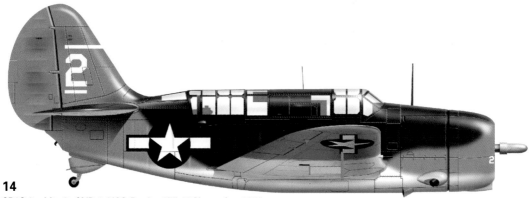

14
SB2C-3 white 2 of VB-4, USS *Bunker Hill*, 13 November 1944

15
SB2C-3 black 3 of VB-20, USS *Enterprise*, 24 November 1944

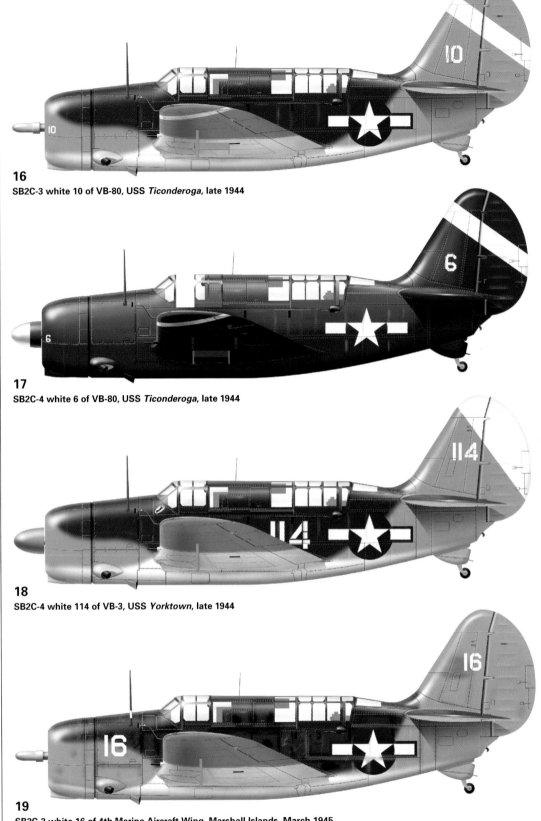

16
SB2C-3 white 10 of VB-80, USS *Ticonderoga*, late 1944

17
SB2C-4 white 6 of VB-80, USS *Ticonderoga*, late 1944

18
SB2C-4 white 114 of VB-3, USS *Yorktown*, late 1944

19
SB2C-3 white 16 of 4th Marine Aircraft Wing, Marshall Islands, March 1945

20
SB2C-3 white 105 of VB-9, USS *Lexington*, 2 March 1945

21
SB2C-4E white 95 of VB-82, USS *Bennington*, February 1945

22
SB2C-4E white 15 of VB-12, USS *Randolph*, February 1945

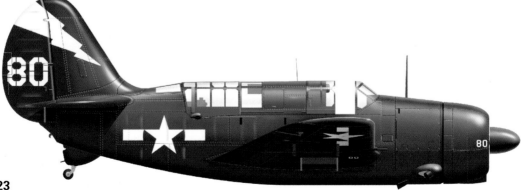

23
SB2C-4 white 80 of VB-85, USS *Shangri-La*, 3 June 1945

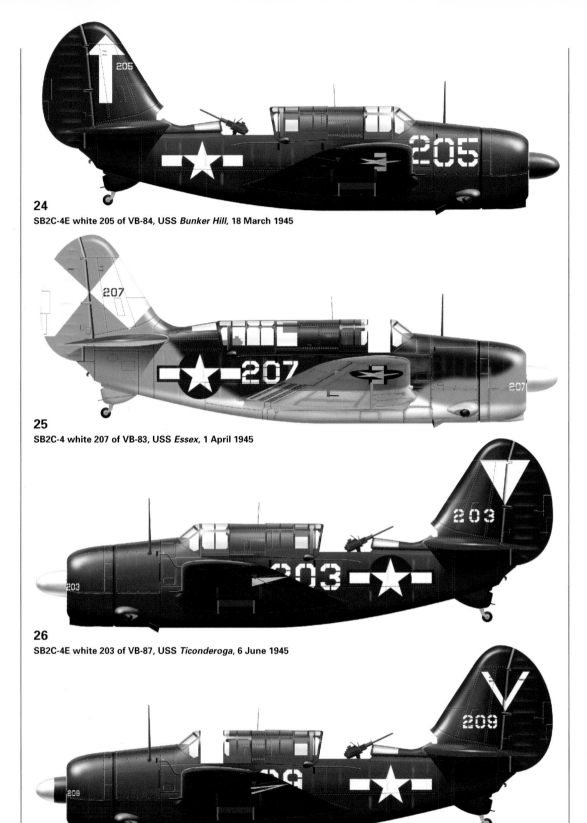

24
SB2C-4E white 205 of VB-84, USS *Bunker Hill*, 18 March 1945

25
SB2C-4 white 207 of VB-83, USS *Essex*, 1 April 1945

26
SB2C-4E white 203 of VB-87, USS *Ticonderoga*, 6 June 1945

27
SB2C-4E white 209 of VB-87, USS *Ticonderoga*, 25 July 1945

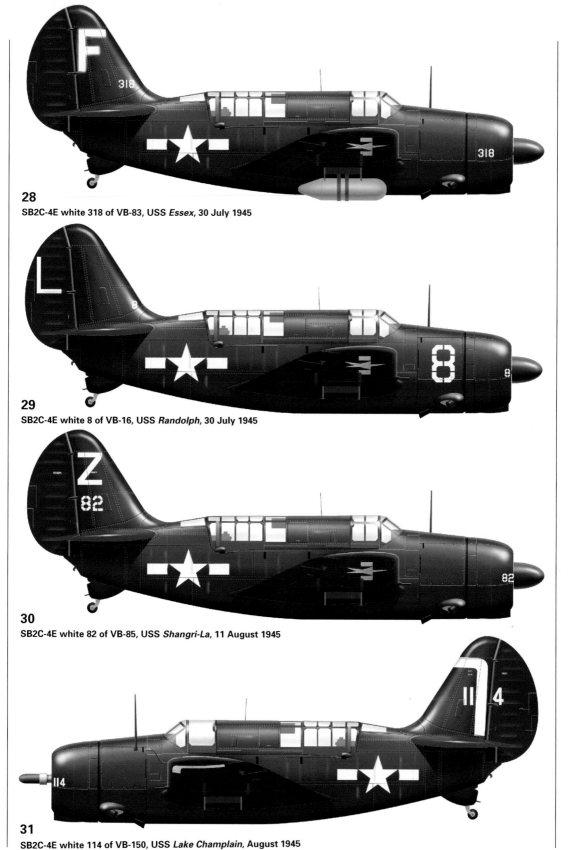

28
SB2C-4E white 318 of VB-83, USS *Essex*, 30 July 1945

29
SB2C-4E white 8 of VB-16, USS *Randolph*, 30 July 1945

30
SB2C-4E white 82 of VB-85, USS *Shangri-La*, 11 August 1945

31
SB2C-4E white 114 of VB-150, USS *Lake Champlain*, August 1945

32
SB2C-5 white 82 of VB-10, USS *Intrepid*, September 1945

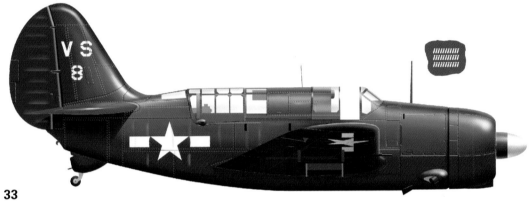

33
SB2C-5 white 8 of the Victory Squadron, October 1945

1
Lt Cdr Richard S McGowan, commanding officer of VB-19 aboard USS *Lexington* (CV-16) in October 1944

2
Enlisted radioman/gunner from a Helldiver unit in the Pacific in 1944

3
Lt Bob Wood, flight (operations) officer, VB-17, NAS Norfolk, Virginia, in mid-1943

TOKYO AND BEYOND

The Japanese home islands had been immune to carrier-launched air attack since the Doolittle raid of April 1942. But nearly three years after 18 B-25s had bombed Tokyo, Yokohama and Nagoya, the US Navy's fast carriers returned to Empire waters in numbers undreamed of by the airmen who launched from *Hornet* (CV-8). On 16-17 February 1945, Task Force 38's 16 carriers embarked more than 1000 modern combat aircraft, including some 135 Helldivers. Amongst the units off the coast of Japan was VB-17 aboard the second *Hornet* (CV-12), this unit returning to combat 11 months after departing *Bunker Hill* upon completion of the first Helldiver deployment.

During the two-day strikes against airfields and other targets on the Tokyo Plain, ten SB2C squadrons also flew searches and anti-submarine patrols. Despite intense aerial combat, Helldivers were intercepted for perhaps the last time ever. On the afternoon of the 16th, VB-9 off *Lexington* scored two fighters damaged while withdrawing from attacks upon the Nakajima Ota aircraft plant.

A similar target was drawn by *Randolph's* (CV-15) aviators. Assigned the Tachikawa Aircraft Engine Plant north-west of Tokyo, Air Group 12

The division leader's rear-seat man took this photo of the remaining five Helldivers in his VB-3 formation. The occasion may be the invasion of Iwo Jima in February 1945, owing to the large number of landing craft and the ordnance load-out, which includes 250-lb bombs on the wing racks (*Tailhook*)

An SB2C-4E prepares for a 'deck run' launch from USS *Bennington* (CV-20) in February 1945. Easily identified by its 'Christmas tree' group symbol, this VB-82 Helldiver carries its AN/APS-4 radar below the port wing, as well as a single high-velocity aerial rocket (HVAR). The squadron remained aboard until mid-June, having participated in the Iwo Jima, home islands and Okinawan operations (*Tailhook*)

found improved weather over land but, according to one VB-12 pilot, 'We were jinking left and right and up and down, and the AA fire was all over the place'. Shortly thereafter, two Bombing 12 gunners combined to shoot up a 'Topsy' transport, which was probably destroyed near Kasumi naval air station. The Helldivers expended most of their remaining ammunition on ships in Tokyo Bay while outbound to the task force.

Shortly before noon the next day a Bombing Three gunner got a shot at an 'Oscar' during strikes on the Tachikawa Engine Plant and claimed a probable kill.

However, these events were rare, as carrier-based Hellcats and Corsairs rolled up awesome victory claims against the Japanese Navy and Air Force. On the first day, 16 February, some 270 shootdowns were credited – the second-highest one-day score ever for Navy fighters, exceeded only the by Marianas Turkey Shoot.

Bombing 17, the first SB2C squadron to see combat, was also the first Helldiver unit to return to the Pacific for a second tour. Embarked in *Hornet* for the 1945 deployment, VB-17 reached Japan itself – these SB2C-3s are preparing to launch against Honshu on 16 February 1945 (*US Navy*)

Only five SB2Cs were lost on 16-17 February, all to operational causes. Three belonged to *Randolph's* VB-12 while the other two were from *Bunker Hill's* VB-84. The following SB2C squadrons were involved in the Tokyo and Iwo Jima operations in February 1945;

VB-3	*Yorktown*	SB2C-3, -4	Cdr J T Lowe
VB-4	*Essex*	SB2C-3	Lt Cdr C V Johnson
VB-9	*Lexington*	SB2C-4	Lt Cdr T F Schneider
VB-12	*Randolph*	SB2C-4E	Lt Cdr R A Embree
VB-17	*Hornet*	SB2C-3	Lt Cdr R M Ware
VB-80	*Hancock*	SB2C-3	Lt Cdr E L Anderson
VB-81	*Wasp*	SB2C-3, SBW-3	Lt Cdr H P Lanham
VB-82	*Bennington*	SB2C-4	Lt Cdr H Wood
VB-84	*Bunker Hill*	SB2C-4	Lt Cdr J P Conn

The same SB2C squadrons provided close air support for three Marine Corps divisions during bitter, bloody, fighting at Iwo Jima. Some 750 miles south of Honshu, the Bonin Islands were considered an important milepost on the road to Tokyo Bay. Seventh Air Force P-51Ds began operating there in March, eventually providing escort to Marianas-based B-29s over the enemy capitol itself.

OKINAWA

For Operation *Iceburg* (the invasion of Okinawa), nine SB2C squadrons were embarked in the fast carriers. By this time nearly all flew new SB2C-4s or radar-equipped -4Es.

Lying 300 miles south-west of Honshu, Okinawa, in the Ryukyu

Bombing 12's unmistakable tail stripes and white ailerons proclaimed it as belonging to the new Essex-class carrier *Randolph* (CV-15). Breaking into combat during strikes against targets on the Tokyo Plain on 16-17 February 1945, VB-12 remained aboard 'Randy' until the end of May (*Tailhook*)

An SB2C-3 of Bombing Squadron Nine during the split cruise of 1945. Originally deployed in *Lexington* from 3 February to 6 March 1945, 'CAG-9' then shifted to *Yorktown* for the remainder of the deployment, which ended on 16 June. The squadron had previously flown Dauntlesses from *Essex* in 1943-44, observing the first anniversary of the major anti-shipping strike against Truk Atoll while bombing targets near Tokyo on 16 February 1945 (*Tailhook*)

This SB2C-4E from VB-85 nosed over upon returning to *Shangri-La* (a new Essex-class carrier) from a bombing raid on Okinawa in May 1945. The lightning bolt tail marking as worn by the units within CVG-85 was one of the most easily recognisable of the late-war period

chain, was the last major stepping stone to Japan proper. There was no doubt that Imperial Headquarters would spare little effort to defend Okinawa from the sea and from the air, as well as ashore. The following units were involved in the Okinawan campaign between April and June 1945;

VB-5	*Franklin*	SB2C-4E	Lt Cdr J G Sheridan
VB-6	*Hancock*	SB2C-3/3E, -4/4E	Lt Cdr G P Chase
VB-9	*Yorktown*	SB2C-4	Lt Cdr T F Schneider
VB-10	*Intrepid*	SB2C-4E	Lt Cdr R B Buchan
VB-17	*Hornet*	SB2C-3, -4	Lt Cdr R M Ware
VB-82	*Bennington*	SB2C-4E	Lt Cdr H Wood
VB-83	*Essex*	SB2C-4	Lt Cdr D R Berry
VB-84	*Bunker Hill*	SB2C-4/4E	Lt Cdr J P Conn
VB-85	*Shangri-La*	SB2C-4E	Lt Cdr A L Maltby, Jr
VB-86	*Wasp*	SB2C-4	Lt Cdr P R Nopby
VB-87	*Ticonderoga*	SB2C-4E	Lt Cdr F N Kanaga

A VB-85 gunner 'bails out' of his aircraft, which has suffered a broken engine mount following a barrier engagement aboard *Shangri-La* on 6 March 1945. Fire crews are dousing the engine and accessory section to prevent a fire igniting from the ruptured fuel lines (*Jim Sullivan*)

The Helldiver squadrons would be hard pressed to meet the various mission requirements for Okinawa. Reduced to 15 aircraft per CV as a result of the *kamikaze* blitz, SB2C crews were briefed for shipping strikes, anti-submarine patrols, support of ground troops and a variety of special-mission functions.

'L' Day at Okinawa was 1 April 1945. Trained in close air support tactics, the bombing squadrons worked with Army and Marine Corps infantry via a sophisticated air support network. Both ground-based and airborne controllers directed bombers to their targets, where troops identified friendly lines by means of coloured panels and smoke. Dive-bomber pilots especially sought precision targets such as Japanese trenches, gun sites, or even individual foxholes.

Although the initial landings were relatively unopposed, few Allied planners felt this situation would last long. They were proven right on two consecutive days – on 6 April one of the largest suicide attacks of

the war was unleashed against the invasion fleet. Carrier-based fighters claimed more than 250 aircraft shot down, while 18 ships were sunk or damaged.

The next day saw the last major air attack on Japanese warships manoeuvring in the open sea. The Imperial Navy despatched the super battleship *Yamato* with a light cruiser and a squadron of destroyers, intending to smash through American and British task groups and beach themselves on Okinawa's north coast. Once there, presumably the stranded warships would become unsinkable batteries of heavy artillery.

Located at sea by Martin PBM Mariners and shadowed by carrier scouts, the *Yamato* force was subjected to attacks by 386 TF-38 aircraft – almost exactly the number of Japanese carrier aircraft which had attacked Pearl Harbor.

Four SB2C squadrons participated – Bombing 9 from *Yorktown*, VB-10 aboard *Intrepid*, VB-83 in *Essex* and VB-84 from *Bunker Hill*. Attack co-ordinators circling over the ten enemy ships assigned targets to each air group – a task somewhat complicated by relatively low ceilings and

Bunker Hill's **ordnancemen prepare a VB-84 'Beast' for another mission on 18 March 1945. By this period in the war, some carriers had begun to use three-digit side numbers, often with the bombing squadron in the 200 realm – despite the fact that an increasing need for air defence had limited most ships to just 15 Helldivers! Bombing 84 participated in the home islands and** *Yamato* **strikes, before** *Bunker Hill* **sustained crippling kamikaze damage on 11 May (***Tailhook***)**

This VB-83 aircraft is seen aboard *Essex* **at the beginning of the Okinawa invasion on 1 April 1945. Reporting aboard in March, VB-83 was still flying from the veteran carrier at the end of hostilities in August (***Tailhook***)**

reduced visibility. Of the Helldiver squadrons, two were directed against *Yamato* herself – VB-83 and VB-10.

The *Essex* aviators came under fire from a variety of anti-aircraft guns, including spectacular air bursts from the battleship's huge 18-in turrets. When the TBM torpedo bombers were in position, the Helldivers nosed down from as low as

6000 ft in a co-ordinated attack meant to split the enemy's defences. In 65° to 80° dives, and releasing at 1500 to 2000 ft, VB-83 reported four direct hits on *Yamato* with armour-piercing bombs.

Meanwhile, Bombing Nine was assigned the light cruiser *Yahagi*. Although one SB2C was shot down during the attack, the *Yorktown* fliers dived from astern and the 13 pilots claimed eight direct hits and five near misses. Regrouping north of the sinking cruiser, the Helldivers circled back and strafed the area en route to rendezvous with the rest of the air group. *Yahagi* finally exploded and sank that afternoon.

Bunker Hill's VB-84 put up ten Helldivers under Lt Cdr John Conn. Searching with his SB2C-4E's radar, he gained contact at 32 miles with visual sighting at 20. Group co-ordination was impossible in low clouds, so Conn's men dived on one of the screening destroyers from 3500 ft. Suppressing anti-aircraft fire, the SB2Cs achieved an unspecified number of direct hits, which were difficult to register in the clouds, smoke and confusion. As VB-84 pulled away, aircrews noted that the ship was down by the stern. Later identified as *Hamakaze*, she also sank.

Among the final squadrons over the target was *Intrepid's* VB-10, one of the senior bombing squadrons in the fleet. With two previous combat deployments in *Enterprise*, the unit was well experienced and went after *Yamato* with a vengeance. A few SB2Cs were damaged by AA fire, but pilots pressed home their attacks and added to the carnage already sustained by the huge battleship.

In all, this last gasp of the once-invincible Imperial Navy cost *Yamato*, *Yahagi* and four destroyers. Seven Helldivers were lost that day, including three from *Hornet's* VB-17 – the 'original' SB2C squadron was now back in combat, led by Lt Cdr R M Ware.

VB-83'S REPORT

VB-83, aboard *Essex*, submitted a report at the end of the Okinawa campaign in June 1945. Since SB2Cs were frequently assigned close air support missions, the squadron's corporate opinion is of interest;

Bombing 83's SB2C-4s exchanged their 'double diamond' air group symbol for the letter 'F' in accordance with a Navy-wide markings change that took effect in July. Note that this Helldiver shows evidence of overspraying on the newly-applied letter

This VB-87 SB2C-4 went into the water near *Ticonderoga* (CV-14) on 6 June 1945. The pilot and gunner are both exiting the sinking Helldiver, which typically floated for two to three minutes, depending upon the amount of fuel remaining in the tanks (*Tailhook*)

'It is not believed that the best possible use was made of carrier bombing squadrons on Okinawan air support missions. The principal difficulties lay in the failure of CASCUs (Close Air Support Control Units) to assign targets early enough, resulting in much orbiting followed by rushed attacks; the inaccurate air support charts and consequent difficulties in locating targets; requests by CASU to "reconnoitre areas and attack targets of opportunity"; and the assignment of towns as targets. It has been noted that two of the most important factors contributing to the success of air support missions are pilot morale and interest. If they have to orbit for an hour-and-a-half and then rush through an attack, or if they are assigned areas such as towns to bomb, their morale drops. They are generally eager to be assigned pin-point targets such as artillery or mortar positions, if they definitely are marked by the air observer or air co-ordinator, and to spend the entire period methodically attacking, dropping one bomb at a time and then strafing. The air co-ordinator should have enough time available to indicate error, or shift the aiming point as necessary. It is suggested that CASCU assign carrier bombing squadrons the most difficult target available, in the belief that the harder the job the better the results will be. Wherever possible, carriers should be informed of potential targets 24 hours in advance in order that there may be some briefing.

'The SB2C loaded is not a good aeroplane for spotting targets. Its turning radius is too large and it is difficult to take the necessary evasive action. It is suggested that target search be assigned (to) fighters.

This Bombing 87 'Beast' had better luck than Number 203 , seen on the previous page, as at least it got back aboard 'Tico' on 25 July despite severe damage. Besides the obvious loss of part of the vertical fin and rudder, the starboard aileron has also come adrift. Note that the previous inverted triangle has given way to the letter 'V', repeated on the tail and on the undersurface of the port wing (*Tailhook*)

With tailhook dangling, VB-87's number 205 apparently bounced on impacting the deck, missed the arresting wires and snared one of the barriers. Two propeller blades are already curled around the steel cables, and the engine cowling has been pushed inward as a result of the impact (*Jim Sullivan*)

'It is also suggested that better results might be obtained if the air co-ordinator for fast carrier support missions land at an airfield, when available, for special briefing by CASCUs.'

During its five months in *Essex*, VB-83 lost 13 pilots or gunners in 9 aircraft. The CO, Lt Cdr David Berry, and his gunner were killed in action during a 13 May strike on Saeki airfield and seaplane base. The worst flak encountered by the unit was over Yokosuka Harbour on 18 July when they attacked the battleship *Nagato*. VB-83 lost Ens Ernest Baker, who was captured, while eight other SB2Cs were downed from the task force.

Air Group 94 Helldivers and Avengers over the Japanese coast during strikes in the summer of 1945. One of the last air groups to enter combat, CVG-94's SB2C-4Es flew from *Lexington* in the final weeks of the war (*US Navy*)

No enemy aircraft intercepted Air Group 83 bombers, so the SB2C gunners only used their twin .30-cal mounts in strafing. More frequently, aircrewmen carried bags of 28-in aluminum foil strips and emptied them overboard when heavy AA fire seemed likely to be radar-controlled.

Post VJ-Day 'bombing' operations were far more pleasant. The squadron loaded bomb bays with food, candy and cigarettes for 'airmail deliveries' to prisoner of war camps in Japan. The gleeful response from the starving, emaciated, PoWs was evident even from the air.

Ironically, an SB2C pilot made a lasting mark on naval aviation in the next war too. On 3 July 1950 two VF-51 aviators flying Grumman F9F-2s from *Valley Forge* (CV-45) downed a pair of North Korean Yak-9s – the first aerial victories by US Navy jets. Lt Leonard Plog, formerly of VB-83, gained the first kill (see Osprey *Aircraft of the Aces 4 - Korean War Aces* for more details).

BUNKER HILL'S AGONY

Helldivers fought their war not only in the air above Japanese fleet units and in the sky over outlying bases or the home islands. For some SB2C squadrons, the worst of the war came at sea, in their own carriers. By far the most dramatic example was Bombing 84's ordeal off Okinawa.

On the morning of 11 May 1945, *Bunker Hill* had set Condition One Easy with ventilators open, drawing fresh air into hot compartments below decks. Meanwhile, 34 aeroplanes were on the flightdeck being prepared for the next launch. Lt J E 'Jug' Barrows led crews from VB-84 towards nine SB2Cs parked aft, while fighter and torpedo pilots also prepared to move their mounts forward so airborne aircraft could land.

At 1005, abrupt screams brought the aviators' attention overhead – a bomb-laden Zeke plunged toward the flightdeck, dropped its bomb, and dived into the F4Us forward. Skidding along the deck, shedding pieces and bursting into flames, the A6M5 splashed into the water to port.

The 550-lb bomb with a delayed-action fuse penetrated the wooden

Bombing Squadron 16 finally took Helldivers into combat after making one of the last two Dauntless cruises from *Lexington* in 1943-44. These SB2C-4Es, bearing *Randolph's* 'L' tail code, are seen cruising past Mount Fuji on 30 July 1945. VB-16 served aboard the latter carrier during the last two months of hostilities, from 17 June to 15 August. That period saw carrier strikes flown against the remainder of the Imperial Japanese Navy, which was largely anchored without fuel in Kure Harbour (*Tailhook*)

planking of the deck and, angling to port, smashed through the thin plates and detonated outside the hull.

VB-84 pilots, who seconds before had intended to taxy forward, now abandoned aircraft and dashed for the starboard catwalk, away from the flames. High-test aviation fuel pouring from shattered Corsairs drenched the deck and ignited in a low, rolling, explosion. Massive flames and a volcano of thick, black, smoke embroiled the ship topsides.

Just as several SB2C pilots reached the safety of the catwalk, they heard a 20 mm mount open fire over their heads, training aft. Glancing upward, the helpless aviators gasped at the sight – a 'Judy' dive-bomber had the ship 'boresighted' from astern.

Like the Zeke mere seconds before, the 'Judy' released its bomb just before impact. The weapon splintered the planking aft of the island – a near-perfect centre hit – and exploded on the gallery deck. The remains of the flak-riddled dive-bomber crashed near the bomb hole – the engine wrenched free of the airframe as a wing was severed on the steel structure of the island.

With the second fire added to the first, *Bunker Hill* was aflame nearly from stem to stern. Witnesses on other ships in the task force gaped at the carnage – it appeared as if a volcano had erupted from within CV-17's agonised hull. Aircraft went up in flames as ordnance 'cooked off'.

The SB2C maintenance officer, Lt Thomas Balzhiser, was conversing with the ship's air operations officer on the bridge. The 'Judy's' wing cut a swath perhaps six feet from the wing of the flight-control bridge, where men were cut by wood splinters and shards of steel.

As 'General Quarters' sounded, Balzhiser dashed for his battle station in the forecastle. But a molten furnace of flame and acrid smoke spewed up the ladder way, forcing him backwards. The engineering officer spun around, collided with Capt Gene Seitz, and finally climbed down the outside of the island, grasping hand holds wherever possible.

Briefly treating another officer's burned hands, Balzhiser crawled along the flight deck to avoid .50-cal ammunition ignited by the heat and flames. At least there was no immediate danger from heavy ordnance, as the SB2Cs had not yet been armed with bombs. Finally, he reached the forecastle, where he continued rendering first aid to an appalling number of casualties. There seemed no end to them.

Meanwhile, other bomber men were fighting their own battle for survival. Working aft, Lt Barrows

Following a 'pit stop' aboard *Independence* (CVL-22), this VB-16 Helldiver heads back to *Randolph* in August 1945. Although capable of operating from light carriers, the SB2C's sheer size prevented sufficient aircraft from being embarked. Therefore, CVL air groups were limited to fighters and torpedo aircraft only (*Jim Sullivan*)

Yet another 'victim' of the air group identification change in July 1945 was VB-85 aboard *Shangri-La*. The letter 'Z' replaced 'Shang's' vivid lightning bolt insignia painted diagonally across the vertical tail. First embarked in *Shangri-La* in November 1944, the air group entered combat during the Okinawa campaign in late April 1945, remaining in the frontline until shortly after the formal surrender on 2 September (*Tailhook*)

found a wooden plank and managed to lodge it between the starboard catwalk and the fantail. Other refugees were gathering there – how many was impossible to tell in the thickening, dense smoke. Some of the men had lowered three or more lines into the water, offering a last-ditch means of escape, but the ship was still underway and the churning wake reminded the men of the danger from the huge propellers. Most of the men decided to await events, trying to preserve some air by tying handkerchiefs or shop rags over their faces.

Though it seemed interminable, the carrier's ordeal was already being met. Light cruiser USS *Wilkes Barre* (CL-103) came alongside to starboard, directing fire hoses toward the burning aircraft on the flightdeck. Almost simultaneously, three destroyers pulled up on the port beam. One of them provided a heaven-sent spray onto the crowded, smoke-clogged, fantail, where men still coughed and gagged in the increasing smoke and steam.

Bad as it was topside, below decks, conditions were a Dantesque hell. It was especially bad in the ready rooms. Some VB-84 fliers managed to fight their way through panicked, struggling, men in the passageway and scrape their way through opened portholes in the hull.

Headed for Kikai Shima's temporary anchorage, *Bunker Hill* fought the flames for more than four hours. Some of the fires had been subdued – few had been extinguished – but lines were passed to the cruiser and 'tin cans' alongside, permitting the transfer of some severely wounded men. Still forward on the flightdeck, Bombing 84's CO, John Conn, began counting his losses. At one point he calculated that he had lost most of his squadron. Then, singly and in small groups, the Helldiver crews began trickling back from the catwalks and fantail.

Below decks the carnage was appalling. Rescue crews found the pas-

USS *Intrepid* (CV-11) was one of very few carriers to retain its 'G' symbol long after the letter tailcode system had been implemented in July 1945. Seen over China in early September, the crew of this VB-10 Helldiver are enjoying a peacetime flight for a change. Bombing 10 was among the most experienced squadrons in the fleet, with previous *Enterprise* cruises in SBDs during 1942 and 44 (*Tailhook*)

Top and above
Another exception to the mid-1945 revision of air group identification was seen in USS *Lake Champlain* (CV-39). Still on the East Coast at the end of the war, 'Champ's' aircraft bore the distinctive marking on wings and tail as seen on these VB-150 Helldivers in August 1945 (*Tailhook*)

sageway outside the ready room for Bombing 84's gunners choked with bodies, as was the passage near the Torpedo 84 room. It appeared that groups of men racing aft had met another crowd surging forward, both seeking to escape smoke and flames. In the dark, smoke, and confusion, men became immobilised until the fumes overcame them.

Combat losses for Air Group 84 had been bad enough, with 29 aircrew killed in action – the two suiciders claimed 103 more. Twenty-one VB-84 men were among the air group dead on 11 May, while Helldiver losses had involved four operational and five to anti-aircraft gunfire, in addition to the 15 aircraft burned on deck.

Finally out of immediate danger, *Bunker Hill* shaped course for the fleet anchorage at Ulithi Atoll. No other squadrons ever flew from her deck.

During July 1945 the heaviest SB2C losses were sustained by VB-16 in *Randolph* (CV-15), with 12 to all causes, both combat and operational. This equated to 80 per cent attrition of their allotted strength.

The following units were in combat on VJ-Day, 15 August 1945.

VB-1	*Bennington*	SB2C-4/4E	Lt M Tyre
VB-6	*Hancock*	SB2C-4E	Lt Cdr G P Chase
VB-16	*Randolph*	SB2C-4E	Lt R N McMackin
VB-83	*Essex*	SB2C-4/4E	Lt Cdr J T Crawford
VB-85	*Shangri-La*	SB2C-4E	Lt Cdr A L Maltby, Jr
VB-86	*Wasp*	SB2C-4/4E	Lt Cdr P R Nopboy
VB-87	*Ticonderoga*	SB2C-4E	Lt Cdr F N Kanaga
VB-88	*Yorktown*	SB2C-4/4E	Lt Cdr J S Elkins
VB-94	*Lexington*	SB2C-4E	Lt Cdr C H Mester

On the last day of hostilities (15 August 1945), VB-6 off *Hancock* (CV-19) recorded the last Helldiver casualty of the war when Ens Edward E Hawks' SB2C-4E was lost at sea.

When Imperial Japan formally surrendered on 2 September, the US Navy had some 48 squadrons equipped with more than 700 Helldivers. From that point on, the 'Beast's' importance to naval aviation steadily declined until, less than four years later, it had disappeared from the carrier decks it had once adorned.

OTHER USERS

In April 1941 Curtiss Model S84 was contracted by the US Army Air Force as the A-25. At the same time the Army purchased Douglas A-24 Banshees based on the SBD Dauntless scout bomber. The USAAF's S84, called the Shrike after a previous Curtiss product, had no carrier-specific equipment such as catapult fittings or tailhooks, and only the first ten were delivered with folding wings. Further modifications included Army radios and a different arrangement for the armour plating.

The Army Air Force ordered 3000 A-25As in early 1942, with the type's first flight in late September. Early production Shrikes retained leading edge wing slats which were subsequently eliminated.

However, by the time SB2Cs entered combat in late 1943 the US Army no longer needed a large, slow, dive-bomber. After 900 Shrikes had been delivered, the Army cast about for a likely repository and offered the aircraft to the Royal Australian Air Force. Following a preliminary evaluation, the RAAF declined. Therefore, the Army provided most of its Shrikes to the Marine Corps, which received 410 A-25As, including about 140 intended for Australia. Of the latter, apparently only ten were actually shipped. The Marines' former USAAF aircraft were designated SB2C-1As, and apparently all were retained for operational training in the continental United States. Monthly location reports of naval aircraft indicate that Marine Corps Helldivers in the Pacific Theatre of Operations were SB2C-3s and -4s, or their SBW equivalents.

Of the 450 Canadian Car SBW-1s built, 26 were delivered to the British Royal Navy as SBW-1Bs. This was barely enough to equip one Fleet Air Arm unit in 1944, and the Helldiver Mk Is never saw combat.

Helldivers began appearing in Marine Corps squadrons in the spring of 1944, first with VMSB-344 at Greenville, in South Carolina, and then

This unidentified Marine Corps Helldiver served with one of the 26 SB2C squadrons equipped with the type between early 1944 and the end of the war. The Marines received hundreds of Army A-25s, redesignated SB2C-1As, for operational training in the United States (*Jim Sullivan*)

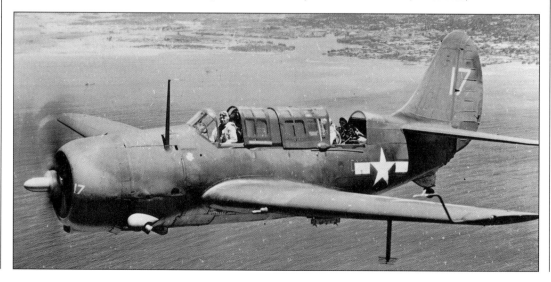

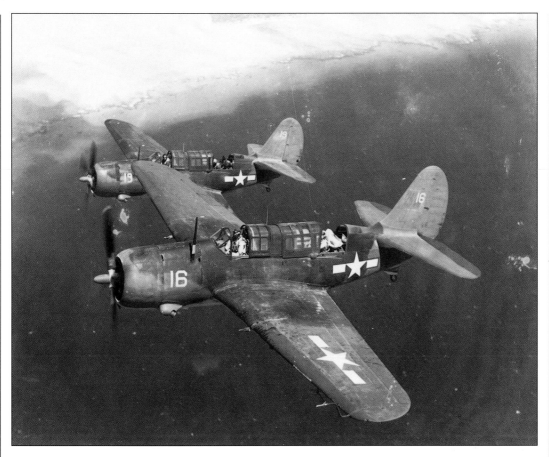

A pair of sunbaked Helldivers from the Fourth Marine Aircraft Wing in the Marshall Islands in March 1945. Two 'Leatherneck' squadrons flew SB2Cs in the Central Pacific at that time, but only VMSB-151 at Engebi Island had 'dash threes' (*Jerry Scutts*)

VMSB-454 at San Diego. Both squadrons had SB2C-1As, former Army Air Force A-25s. One of the first 'leatherneck' Helldiver squadrons deployed to the Pacific was Maj R J Shelley's VMSB-151 with 28 'dash threes', who were sent to Engebi, in the Marshall Islands.

Marine Corps aircraft groups were committed to the Philippines campaign beginning in late 1944, supporting both 'leathernecks' and US Army troops. Marine units were based on the main island of Leyte, as well as Mindanao, southernmost of the major Philippine islands. On the latter island, three primary fields were used – Dipolog on the north coast, Malabang on Illana Bay and Zamboanga at the tip of the western peninsula.

The nearly 300 aircraft under 'MAGZAM' (Marine Aircraft Group, Zamboanga) were comprised of four primary types – 151 Douglas SBD Dauntlesses, 96 Vought/Goodyear F4U/FG Corsairs, 18 North American PBJ Mitchells and 18 SB2Cs. The latter were the 'Bombing Banshees' of VMSB-244, which arrived in the Philippines in December 1944 and received Helldivers in late May 1945. The 'Banshees' finally entered combat by attacking Cabagulo, on Mindanao, on 2 June, Maj Vance H Hudgins' crews flying in support of the Army's Tenth Corps during this period.

On one of their early SB2C missions, eight of Hudgins' squadron were directed to attack a large building near Davao. They all missed the target, but a 'post strike report' by one of the pilots eliminated any need for con-

cern – he stated that he pulled out so low that he could look through the windows and see nothing left inside!

The commanding general of the corps' 31st Division expressed appreciation for the Marines' support. He said in part, 'The terrain, with its dense jungles and precipitous mountains, the tops frequently being obscured by clouds, made flying extremely hazardous for the pilots and crews. Some of the targets were located in positions which were surrounded by many steep-sloped, jutting, mountain peaks which made dive bombing both difficult and dangerous. Although air units have the prerogative of refusing to fly missions involving unjustified risks to aircraft and personnel, there was never a refusal.'

Hudgins' unit was the last dive-bomber squadron left in Marine Air Group 24 at war's end, the two Dauntless squadrons having been disestablished in mid-July.

The Marine Corps operated 25 Helldiver squadrons during World War 2, with a peak strength of some 300 aircraft in April 1945. At war's end the total included five squadrons west of Hawaii – VMSB-343 at Midway, -231, -245 and -331 in the Central Pacific, and -244 in the Philippines. Two more were based in Hawaii, with eight on the West Coast and ten more in the Eastern United States. Of the Marines' 'stateside' Helldiver squadrons, most were replacement or operational training units. According to location and allowance reports, the majority of their aircraft were SB2C-1As or SBW-3s and -4s.

From November 1944 through to August 1945, Marine Helldiver squadrons lost 18 SB2Cs and SBWs to all causes. VMSB-331 sustained four and -231 three while operating in the Marshall Islands, while -244 lost three in the Philippines during June 1945.

In the 'backwater' of the Pacific Theatre, Helldivers of the 4th Marine Aircraft Wing flew a surprising variety of missions in 1945. Based on VMSB-231 flight logs from April through to July, 'leatherneck' SB2Cs

Aircraft number 19, as seen in the photo on the previous page, is almost certainly a VMSB-151 SB2C-3, with its crudely-painted identification number placed in the unusual location of just behind the cowl flaps (*Jim Sullivan*)

flew a high percentage of practise missions between actual strikes against bypassed Japanese garrisons in the Marshall Islands. One pilot logged 80 flights in those four months, of which just 19 were offensive missions against the enemy. The others were largely training flights, including dive and glide bombing, rocket and strafing practise, and even anti-submarine tactics. Monthly flight time varied between 27 and 46 hours, with the average flight lasting 1.6 hours.

A-25A Shrikes continued in backwater use with the Army Air Force, including a number flown by the 13th Fighter Squadron in Florida and the Panama Canal Zone.

MARINE CORPS HELLDIVER SQUADRONS, JUNE 1945

VMSB-151	Marshall Islands	Lt Col J P Coursey	SBW-3
VMSB-231	Marshall Islands	Maj J W White, Jr	SB2C-4
VMSB-244	Philippine Islands	Maj V H Hudgins	SB2C-4
VMSB-245	Ulithi Atoll	Maj R F Halladay	SBW-3
VMSB-331	Marshall Islands	Maj W E Jewson	SB2C-4E
VMSB-333	Hawaii	Maj L M Williamson	SB2C-4
VMSB-343	Midway Atoll	Maj W E Gregory	SB2C-3
VMSB-464	El Toro, California	Maj E P Paris, Jr	SB2C-4E4
VMSB-474	El Toro, California	Maj W J Carr, Jr	SB2C-4
VMSB-484	El Toro, California	Maj G D Wolverton	SB2C-4/4E
VMSB-931	Oak Grove, La	Capt R W Johannesen	SB2C-4/4E
VMSB-932	Oak Grove, La	Capt E C Willard	SB2C-4/4E
VMSB-933	Bogue Field, NC	Maj E R Hemingway	SB2C-4E
VMSB-934	Bogue Field, NC	Maj E R Polgrean	SB2C-4E

PREVIOUS MARINE CORPS HELLDIVER SQUADRONS

VMSB-132	El Toro, California	October 1944
VMSB-144	El Toro, California	June-November 1944
VMSB-234	El Toro, California	August-October 1944
VMSB-332	Hawaii	September 1944-March 1945 *
VMSB-334	Newport, Arkansas	April 1944
VMSB-342	Newport, Arkansas	April 1944
VMSB-344	Newport, Arkansas	March 1944
VMSB-454	El Toro, California	March-November 1944 *
VMSB-941	Bogue, N Carolina	September-October 1944
VMSB-942	Bogue, N Carolina	September-October 1944
VMSB-943	El Toro, California	November 1944-May 1945 *

* Redesignated VTMB and received TBM Avengers

During the summer of 1945, at least six Marine fighting squadrons were wholly equipped with SB2C-4Es during 'turnaround' training. Based at MCAS El Centro, California, the former Corsair units were VMF-112, -123, -214, -221, -451 and -452. They soon reverted to Vought F4Us and Goodyear FGs following VJ-Day.

SB2C IN PERSPECTIVE

T he SB2C's wartime success was gained against greater odds than most combat aircraft. Burdened with a flawed design, and following an unusually troubled 'incubation' period, the Helldiver overcame most of its original deficiencies to become not merely an adequate dive-bomber, but one regarded with affection by most of its airmen. Today, separated by a half century from the hard reality of combat, pilots and gunners still lament the shortcomings of the SB2C-1 and -1C, while relishing the improvements in the -3 and -4 versions.

Like every other military aircraft, the Helldiver was a means to an end – the end being delivery of ordnance against enemy targets. The strengths and weaknesses of the type in a variety of aspects are examined below.

ARMAMENT

Original armament for the XSB2C-1 was two .30-cal machine guns, firing through the propeller arc from the cowling, and a brace of .50-cals in the rear cockpit. On the initial production batch, the nose-mounted .30s were deleted, and the first 200 production 'dash ones' had four .50-cals in the wings instead, but heavier firepower was still desired, so subsequent Helldivers were fitted with two 20 mm cannon. The latter modification was indicated by the SB2C-1C designation, which was by far the most common fleet Helldiver until the arrival of the 'dash three' in early 1944.

The 20 mm cannon were considered with ambivalence by many Helldiver pilots. The offensive potential was considerable, but reliablity seems to have lagged prior to the SB2C-4. Squadrons reported experiencing 'a great deal of difficulty' with the wing guns, and in some instances failure to fire was more common than not. One major cause of the problem was little or no work by pool ordnancemen to 'depreserve' the cannon – ie, remove the cosmoline grease used to prevent rust.

Otherwise, well-maintained cannon worked fine. In a typical late-war squadron, data for nearly 800 cannon-firing sorties indicated a failure to fire of three per cent, and permanent stoppages of about six per cent. Malfunctions were generally caused by imporper seating of the feed mechanism, link jams and high-G pull-out jams.

Throughout most of the production cycle, the radioman-gunner had twin .30-cal guns fixed on a swivel mount. However, his guns could only be deployed by lowering the rear deck of the fuselage immediately ahead of the vertical stabiliser. It was similar to comparable arrangements on other Curtiss aircraft such as the SOC floatplane and SBC, the biplane which had previously carried the Helldiver name.

An early design concept called for a power-operated turret, somewhat comparable to that fitted to the Grumman TBF Avenger. However, the weight penalty incurred by its fitment was severe, causing the concept to be dropped. A lingering problem was inherited by SBWs, however, as the hydraulic lines to the turret were retained in most production aircraft as a means of expediting delivery. Recalled a VB-3 aircrewman, 'When Canadian Car and Foundry built the SBW, they put in all the hydraulic tubing that would have been needed for the turret, and capped off the lines. The result was that the SBW was a flying hydraulic leak!'

Partly owing to different mission requirements, partly to engineering, the Army version had a lighter armament of four .50-cal. wing guns instead of two 20 mm cannon, and a single .50-cal for the gunner, rather than the Navy's twin .30-cal mount. Curtiss' St Louis, Missouri, factory rolled out 900 examples, although actual Army use was almost wholly limited to utility and 'hack' purposes.

Another gun feature was the twin .30-cal pod which could be suspended from external racks below each wing. Evidence is sketchy, but indicates that the pod was seldom used. However, owing to the relatively limited ammunition capacity for the two 20 mm cannon, the additional fire power of two pods (four machine guns) was a useful option for specific mission functions.

The next model with upgraded armament was the SB2C-3, with four zero-length rocket rails beneath each wing.

Helldivers were capable of a variety of ordnance loads internally – two 500-lb bombs, one 1000 'pounder', one 1600-lb armour-piercing bomb, or three cluster bombs of six 20-lb weapons each.

Bomb bay doors could also be removed in order to install a 2000-lb aerial torpedo. The latter was suspended from a special support attached to

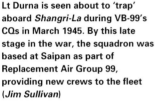

Lt Durna is seen about to 'trap' aboard *Shangri-La* during VB-99's CQs in March 1945. By this late stage in the war, the squadron was based at Saipan as part of Replacement Air Group 99, providing new crews to the fleet (*Jim Sullivan*)

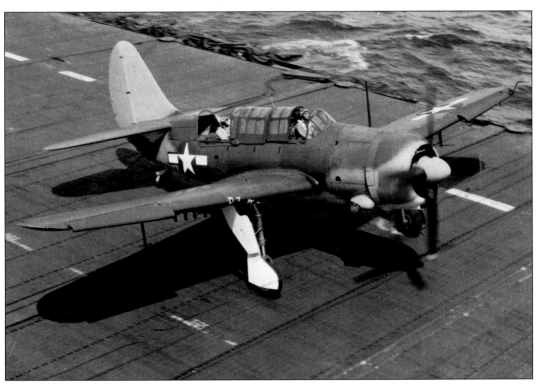

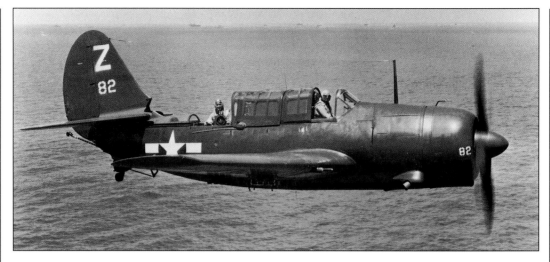

the fuselage outboard bomb racks and the displacing gear fittings on the firewall. However, the Helldiver apparently was never used as a torpedo carrier in combat, largely because Avengers were readily available.

Provision also was made for two 325-lb depth charges, two 100-lb demolition bombs, or two cluster bombs beneath the wings. Far less seldom affixed were two 325-lb smoke tanks, or ten 3-lb practice bombs, again mounted externally.

CAMOUFLAGE AND MARKINGS

Much like the Grumman Hellcat, the SB2C's overall paint schemes reflected the US Navy's operational requirements from 1943 through to 1945. The SB2C-1s and -3s (and early 'dash fours') were delivered in the classic three-tone camouflage for naval aircraft of the 1943-44 period – dark blue upper surfaces, medium-blue fuselage sides and insignia white undersurfaces, with the exception of the bottom of the outer wing panels. The latter were also dark blue, presenting a uniform appearance from overhead when the wings were folded. Usually there was a degree of 'feathering' to blend the demarcation lines between any two colours.

The huge majority of SB2C-4s, and all -5 series aircraft, received the 1944-45 overall dark gloss blue scheme. Thus, the late-model Helldivers appeared in the same uniform colour as F6F-5 Hellcats and most F4U/FG-1D Corsairs, as well as most of the latter production blocks of TBM-3 Avengers.

Insignia red was applied to the insides of the SB2C's dive brakes and generally to the interior of other moving parts. Propeller blades were flat black with yellow tips, and some Helldiver variants with prop spinners occasionally had these painted in distinctive colours as a further means of unit identification.

Those A-25As delivered to the Marine Corps often retained their Army Air Forces olive-drab upper and medium grey undersurfaces.

Three types of national insignia were employed on SB2Cs in fleet service. Those aircraft in the original production batch received the round insignia blue background with white star superimposed, usually on top and bottom of both wings, in addition to each side of the fuselage.

In late 1943 the white horizontal bars were added, with a short-lived

A photo opportunity arose during VB-85's activities of 11 August 1945, just four days before the cessation of hostilities. Bearing its new letter tail identification, this SB2C-4E cruises with the radioman-gunner ready to snap a reciprocal shot of the aircraft that took this picture (*Jim Sullivan*)

red border. This version was applied in the standard four positions, including upper port wing and lower starboard.

The final wartime version deleted the red surround in place of continuing the insignia blue border. When applied on overall gloss blue aircraft, the background often seemed to disappear, giving the impression of the 'star and bar' superimposed upon the fuselage or wing surface.

Another operational marking – although relatively short-lived among fleet SB2Cs – were 'LSO stripes' on the vertical stabiliser. Either in one or two-chevron patterns, they were calculated to help the landing signal officer judge the aircraft's correct attitude as it approached the flightdeck.

Occasionally special-purpose markings were applied for a specific operation. The best example occurred during Task Force 38's initial strikes on the Japanese home islands in February 1945, when each carrier-based aircraft received either a yellow or white recognition band on the front of the engine cowling. These markings were usually short-lived, being intended only for a particular period.

Unit markings came in some variety for SB2C squadrons. Beginning in 1943, and continuing into 1945, squadrons in the United States often used the pre-war alpha-numeric type of designations. For instance, the commanding officer of Bombing Squadron 17 displayed the legend 17-B-1 on his fuselage, ahead of the star. Invariably, these markings were applied in white block letters, with the individual aircraft number often repeated on the cowling and on the landing gear doors in black or white, depending upon the amount of contrast desired.

Individual aircraft numbers within an air group followed approximate patterns through most of 1944. Depending on whether the allocation called for 36 fighters or 54, the Hellcats aboard a given *Essex*-class carrier

Distinctive vertical stripes identified Air Group 89 aboard the new carrier *Antietam* (CV-36) at war's end. VB-89 was among the first squadrons to take SB2C-5s on cruise, while VBF-89's F4U-4s line the starboard side of the flightdeck in this immediate postwar photo (*Jim Sullivan*)

usually received the lower numbers, with dive-bombers taking up the sequence. Bombing Two aboard *Hornet* is an example, with Helldivers in the 41 to 73 range. However, at the same time *Bunker Hill* and *Wasp* assigned numbers 1 through 36 to the bombing squadrons – VB-8 and VB-14, respectively.

Then, in early 1945, several carriers adopted a three-digit number series. Typically, the fighters used the 100 sequence, the dive-bombers 200, and the torpedo squadron was given the 300 range. Whereas F6Fs and F4Us could run up well into the 170 realm, Helldivers were more likely to be found wearing 201 to 215 owing to the fact that there were far fewer of them aboard.

Once assigned to an aircraft carrier, the aircraft within an air group received identical tail markings, or 'G' symbols, with few exceptions. These were geometric shapes easily recognised in combat, ranging from simple stripes and bands to patterns such as arrows, triangles and circles. Among the exceptions were the aircraft of Air Group 19, embarked in USS *Lexington* (CV-16) in the latter part of 1944. The Bombing 19 Helldivers had extremely large individual numbers on the vertical tails, while VF-19 Hellcats used numbers behind the cockpit and Torpedo 19 Avengers employed an inverted triangle.

Beginning in July 1945, each carrier was assigned a one- or two-digit identifying letter. *Essex* (CV-9), for instance, replaced its 'double diamond' design with the letter F, while *Yorktown's* (CV-10) traditional angled stripe became RR.

US Navy Aircraft Carrier Identification Letters – 27 July 1945*

AA	*Lake Champlain* (CV-39)	Air Group 150
E	*Intrepid* (CV-11)	Air Group 10
F	*Essex* (CV-9)	Air Group 83
H	*Lexington* (CV-16)	Air Group 94
L	*Randolph* (CV-15)	Air Group 16
RR	*Yorktown* (CV-10)	Air Group 88
S	*Hornet* (CV-12)	No air group aboard
TT	*Bennington* (CV-20)	Air Group 1
U	*Hancock* (CV-19)	Air Group 6
V	*Ticonderoga* (CV-14)	Air Group 87
W	*Antietam* (CV-36)	Air Group 89
X	*Wasp* (CV-18)	Air Group 86
Y	*Bunker Hill* (CV-17)	No air group aboard
Z	*Shangri-La* (CV-38)	Air Group 85
ZZ	*Boxer* (CV-21)	Air Group 93

* only ships with SB2C squadrons assigned are listed

Not all of these carriers were engaged in combat when the new ID letters took effect, but the system proved sufficient until changed nearly 18 months later.

Unit badges and individual markings were fairly unusual in war zones. However, it was not unusual for a pilot and aircrewman's name to be stencilled below their respective cockpits, even though that crew might never fly their 'assigned' Helldiver during the course of a combat deployment. In the first place, there were always more aircrew than embarked aircraft, and secondly, it was simply not possible to 'spot' a particular aircraft in the appropriate position on the flightdeck for every launch.

However, a few Helldiver squadrons seem to have condoned aircraft names. One such was Bombing Seven aboard *Hancock*, whose SB2Cs sported individual identities painted in white script, such as 'Satan's Angel', seen on page 47.

THE COMMAND VIEW
Dive-bombing Doctrine

By late 1944 the US Navy could draw upon a wealth of institutional experience in the combat use of dive-bombers. One of the documents addressing the subject was *Current Tactical Orders and Doctrine, US Fleet Aircraft* (USF 74B), released in November 1944.

The dive-bombing segment began, 'The rapid and accurate delivery of heavy bombs on the target is the ultimate of performance in dive-bombing. Adherence to and practice of the principles discussed herein should result in attainment of a satisfactorily high degree of proficiency'.

That generic statement preceded 12 pages of detailed descriptions of scout-bomber missions, including glide and low-level attacks, fire distribution and target designation.

Primary factors effecting a dive-bombing mission were weather, enemy interceptors, and enemy anti-aircraft gunfire. Typically, dive-bombers approached a target some 10,000 ft above the torpedo aircraft, while close and 'roving' escort was provided by fighters.

The actual attack often occurred in two phases – a shallow approach from about 20,000 ft, and entry into the final dive some 5000 to 8000 ft lower. Individual aircraft nosed into their attacks with 400-ft intervals between bombers, each successive section or division stepped down. A 'stepped up' formation usually blocked trailing aircrafts' view of the target. Pilots were cautioned against beginning the final dive too soon, lest the flight path become too shallow to be effective.

An 18-aircraft squadron attack involving three six-aeroplane divisions (each with two sections of three) would ideally saturate the defences by simultaneous approaches from left, right and overhead.

In some instances, the wingmen in a section used a technique called 'drop on lead'. When the leader released his bomb after careful aiming, so did the other pilots in the formation. The only advantage of this procedure was reduced exposure to the defences, otherwise much better accuracy was obtained by individual dives. As doctrine stated, 'the single-aircraft attack, producing a continuous rain of bombs at intervals of two to eight seconds, and presenting the enemy gunners a confusing multiplicity of targets, is more destructive to enemy morale and is on the whole more effective.'

After dropping the bomb, usually at 1500 to 2000 ft, aircraft made a high-speed retirement, while varying heading and altitude to compound tracking by enemy gunners.

Glide bombing was generally done in 45° to 55° descents, without the use of dive brakes. These attacks were usually dictated by low cloud cover, darkness, or specialised attacks on hostile submarines. Delayed-action fuses were necessary to avoid the bomber being caught in its own 'frag pattern'. While easier to accomplish than true dive-bombing, the glide tended to exaggerate range errors due to the shallower approach angle.

As a general rule, an 18-aeroplane squadron would normally be assigned to a single high-value target such as a battleship or aircraft carrier. The squadron commander, or strike leader, might delegate a similar force against two heavy or three light cruisers or, rarely, six destroyers.

One of the Navy's most experienced dive-bomber pilots was then-Lt Martin 'Red' Carmody, who flew SBDs from *Enterprise* in 1942-43 and then VB-8's Helldivers aboard *Bunker Hill* in 1944. His appraisal of the dive-bombing mission is based on the dozens of combat sorties that he successfully completed;

'There was nothing glamorous about flying dive-bombers, particularly when you had to contend with the heavy flak around every target. To be accurate in placing one's bomb it was necessary to dive right in over a target where one could be certain of making a 65° to 70° dive. Any dive less than 65° invited trouble, because AA guns increased in accuracy at lower angles of approach. By diving steep, one could more accurately gauge the wind effect and ship's movement, and make a sight adjustment accordingly.

'To be effective in bombing with the SB2C and still pull out without hitting the water/ground, it was necessary to release at about 1500 to 2000 ft altitude. Accuracy decreased for every foot above that. We lost one of our flight leaders over Davao, Philippine Islands, because he began the attack before reaching a position for a steep dive on the target.'

THE OFFICIAL VIEW

The Navy's attitude toward dive-bombers generally, and the SB2C specifically, changed considerably over a two-year period. At first greeted with a great deal of enthusiasm, the Helldiver was expected not only to replace the SBD Dauntless, but to exceed it by a wide margin. Original Bureau of Aeronatics design specifications called for greater range with twice the SBD's bomb load and as much as 60 mph more speed.

In fleet use, the Helldiver typically gave 35 mph more top speed than the Dauntless, with about 20 mph faster cruise. The SB2C's Curtiss-Electric propeller was a frequent source of maintenance problems, as was the 'Beast's' vastly more complex hydraulic system.

Perhaps the Helldiver's main advantage over the Dauntless was folding wings. The SBD was not designed with a requirement for greater numbers than two 18-aeroplane squadrons, with similar-sized fighting and torpedo units. Conversely, as many as 40 SB2Cs were embarked in *Essex*-class carriers at one time. But the quality of the new aircraft seldom matched its quantity in early use.

As a dive-bomber, the -2C could be accurate, but pilots found they had to work harder, especially in the early phase of a dive. The SBD's well-balanced ailerons made corrections relatively easy, but in some conditions the Helldiver tended to accelerate, even with dive brakes extended. Greater air pressure on the control surfaces meant more difficulty keeping on target, or returning to the desired aiming point once put off.

Putting aside operational concerns, a fleet carrier's SB2C role was dependent upon the period in which it was engaged. When VB-17 inaugurated the type to combat in late 1943, the allotted complement was 36 aircraft. However, as air defence requirements increased, fighter squadrons aboard large carriers grew from 36 to 54 and finally to 73 aircraft by early 1945. With limited deck space in even the largest carriers of the era, something had to give. That something was SB2Cs, which decreased numerically to 24 and finally to 15 aircraft per squadron. The theory was impeccable – only Avengers could perform torpedo attacks (SB2Cs never used that option in combat), while Corsairs and Hellcats were increasingly capable of high- and low-angle bombing.

At the time of the Philippine Sea battle in June 1944, the five embarked SB2C squadrons averaged 35 aircraft apiece. The two remaining Dauntless units averaged 27.

Despite the decreasing requirement for dive-bombers in the fleet (especially after Leyte Gulf in October 1944), the Navy continued purchasing large numbers of SB2Cs. Navy air staff training officers on the West Coast of the United States quickly recognised the trend, and adjusted the fighter training syllabus accordingly. Thus, replacement air groups were arriving in *WestPac* with increased offensive capability from their fighter squadrons, but the SB2C pipeline had not been reduced.

Eventually, the facts became known – Curtiss-Wright, politically astute and well connected in Washington, DC, had the ear of some influential individuals in Congress and the Navy Department. Therefore, while Helldivers were being 'beached' at Ulithi, and elsewhere, to make room for Grumman and Vought aircraft, Curtiss continued high-rate production of late-model SB2Cs.

Aside from the 'mission beyond darkness', which resulted in 43 Helldiver losses, the next greatest one-day figures were 20 SB2Cs on 25 October 1944 in the Battle of Leyte Gulf, 21 during combat and suicide attacks off Japan on 19 March 1945 and 24 aboard two replenishment escort carriers during a typhoon on 18 December 1944.

Helldiver losses were largely offset by increased production as the war progressed. Basically, attrition took two forms – combat/operational, and administrative. As the war neared its end, large numbers of SB2Cs were stricken from the record – generally 'dash one's and 'dash threes', as SB2C-4s and -5s rolled off the assembly line. For instance, throughout 1944 some 607 Helldivers were lost to all causes. During the seven-and-a-half months of hostilities in 1945, the figure was 496, although that number included more than 80 'war wearies' scrapped at Pearl Harbor and in other aircraft pools.

In fleet operations, the heaviest losses were sustained in June and October 1944, with 97 and 136 write-offs, respectively. Not surprisingly, those months saw the Marianas battle and the clash in Leyte Gulf.

Apart from losses, even the Navy's senior leaders admitted that the SB2C fell short of original expectations. In a report released in June 1945, Assistant Secretary of the Navy for Air Artemus L Gates conceded, 'When we needed the SB2C neither we nor it was ready. Thanks to the spirit of our people and our airplanes, we won a war with our mistakes as well as with our victories'.

Throughout its 22 months of Pacific combat, the Helldiver logged 18,808 action sorties with the Navy and Marine Corps. Official statistics compiled after the war indicated the loss of 271 to anti-aircraft fire and 18

to enemy aircraft, although monthly returns show barely 60 shot down by enemy AA gunners. This discrepancy may partly be explained by additional categories in the periodic compilations, including aircraft jettisoned with heavy battle damage or stricken with damage beyond repair. In any event, the large majority of such write-offs would have been due to flak damage.

SB2C-5s and F4U-4s of Air Group 75 overfly their newly-delivered home, USS *Franklin D Roosevelt* (CVB-42), in mid-1946

This SB2C-4E was used for test and evaluation work at NAAS Patuxent River in 1946. Note the F8F Bearcat parked behind it

POSTWAR

Meanwhile, Curtiss-Wright's influence extended beyond replacement of attrition aircraft. In 1945, Douglas engineers and managers bitterly noted that their new BT2D-1 single-seat attack aircraft (later famous as the AD Skyraider in Korea and the A-1 in Vietnam) was being limited by their competitor. Wright Aeronautical Corporation built the R-3350 selected to power the Skyraider, and the company attempted to have its own engine derated to less horsepower than originally capable – surely the height of irony!

This SBF-4E hailed from VT-75, part of 'FDR's' Air Group in 1946

By 1945 the SB2C was Curtiss-Wright's primary product. The long-lived P-40 series, built to the tune of some 13,000 airframes, was well past its combat prime. The twin-engine C-46/R5C transport was falling behind Douglas multi-engine types such as the C-54, and the postwar situation looked bleak. Indeed, Curtiss-Wright finally succumbed to corporate oblivion, while its main competitors, Douglas and North American, went on to even greater success in the jet age.

The last operational Helldivers reported in US Navy service were the SB2C-5s of Attack Squadron 54 (VA-54) in June 1949.

The SB2C's career lasted a few more years in the service of five other nations – France, Greece, Italy, Portugal and Thailand. Constitutional developments in Italy in the immediate postwar years prohibited the use of bomber aircraft, so America's military assistance programme in Rome decided to redesignate 40 'S2C-5s'. Arriving in the fall of 1950, the Helldivers eventually equipped two groups based variously at Grottaglie Airfield, Taranto Naval Base, and briefly on Malta. An internal dispute on the control of aviation resulted in half the crews being air force and half navy.

This SB2C-5 (BuNo 83589), seen at an airshow in 1974, is presently the sole airworthy example of the 'Beast', and is owned and flown by the Confederate Air Force in Texas. Badly damaged in a flying accident at its owner's Harlingen, Texas, home, in August 1985, the Helldiver was rebuilt over a three-year period and flown once again in September 1988. A total of 12 Helldivers have survived into the late 1990s – five C-5s, three C-1s, two C-3s and two A-25As. Nine of these reside in America, and single examples can be found in France, Greece and Thailand

The primary mission was anti-submarine patrol, but with the acquisition of twin-engind Lockheed PV-2 Harpoons and Grumman S2F-1 Trackers, the Helldivers finally reverted to the attack role. However, maintenance and supply problems eventually forced the S2Cs into utility work. By the time they were retired in 1959, no fewer than 15 had been lost in accidents.

The Greek Navy received some SB2Cs which remained active until 1953, but the last of the type in combat belonged to France and Thailand. Engaged in the first phase of the Indochina war, French Navy Helldivers from the light carrier *Arromanches* participated in the ill-fated defence of Dien Bien Phu in 1954. The big Curtiss dive-bombers disappeared from their final arena the following year.

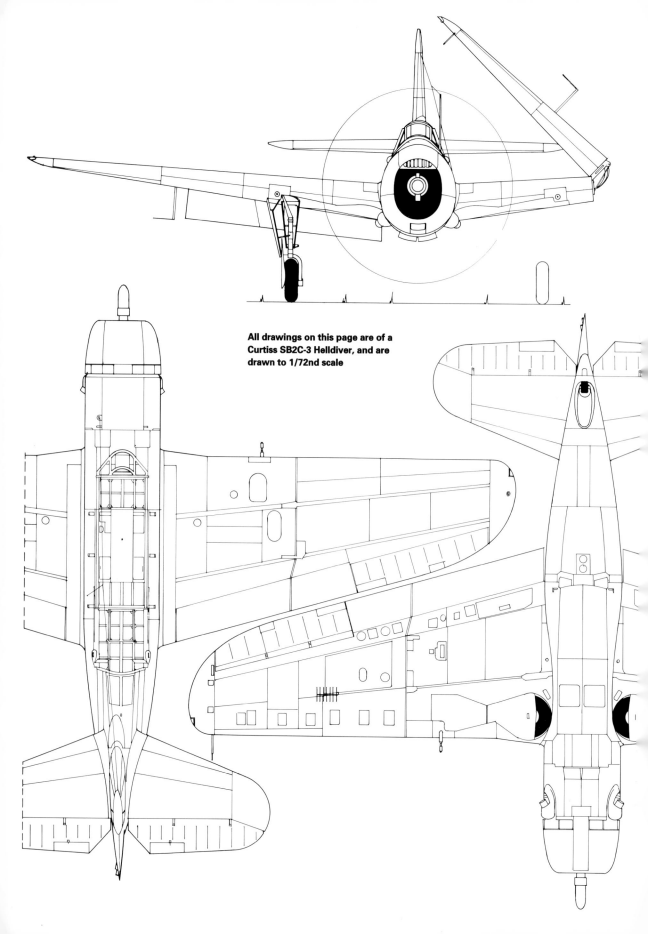

All drawings on this page are of a
Curtiss SB2C-3 Helldiver, and are
drawn to 1/72nd scale

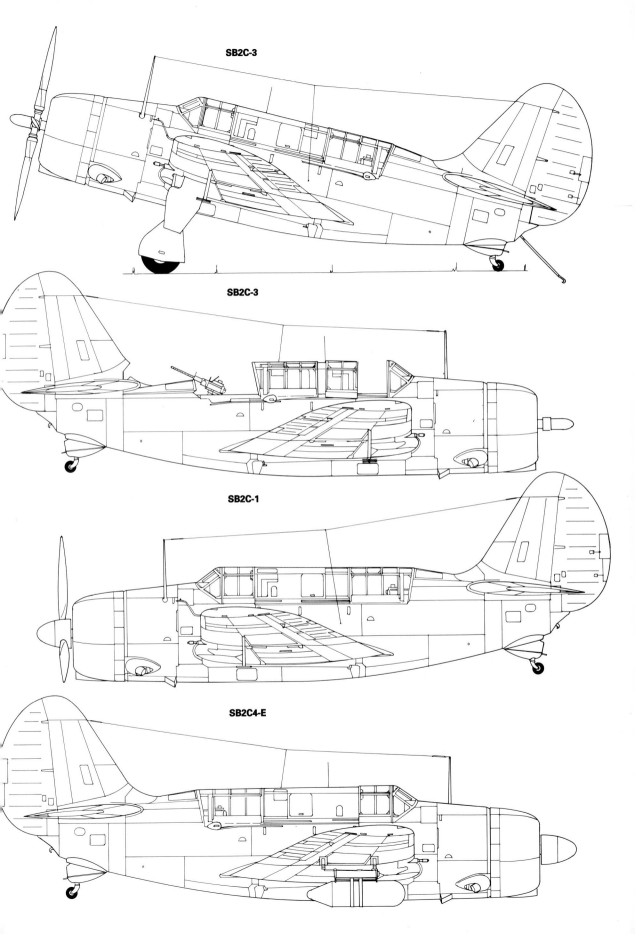

SB2C-3

SB2C-3

SB2C-1

SB2C4-E

COLOUR PLATES

1

SB2C-1 white 17-B-1 of VB-17, USS *Bunker Hill*, July 1943

The first Helldiver squadron to deploy with the new scout-bomber, VB-17 was led by Lt Cdr J E 'Moe' Vose, previously an SBD pilot in USS *Hornet* (CV-8). 'Baker 1' is typical of the mid-1943 transition period in markings, with the then-new tricolour paint scheme and previous national insignia. The full squadron designation on the fuselage was changed in favour of a single number upon deployment. Other operational markings include the dual-chevron LSO stripes on the vertical stabiliser, which provided a visual reference for the LSO to judge the aircraft's proper attitude in the final approach to the deck. The practice was largely discontinued by 1944. VB-17's maiden combat cruise in *Bunker Hill* (CV-17) lasted from November 1943 to March 1944.

2

SB2C-1C white 8-B-16 of VB-8, East Coast, late 1943

Markings still in transition, this Bombing Eight aircraft bears the late 1943 addition of horizontal bars to the US national insignia, but with the short-lived red surround. The latter was subsequently deleted, as it was feared that any red markings would confuse some observers in areas where the Japanese 'meatball' (*hinomaru*) was encountered. The pre-war-style legend 8-B-16 was retained in 'Stateside' carrier squadrons for most of the war, but was removed once the air group was bound for combat. VB-8 flew from USS *Bunker Hill* between March and October 1944, finally rotating home at the start of the Philippines campaign.

3

SB2C-3 white 7 of VB-15, USS *Essex*, 20 May 1944

One of the most active combat deployments of all SB2C squadrons was VB-15's tenure in *Essex* (CV-9) from May to November 1944. Beginning at Marcus Island, Lt Cdr James Mini's Helldivers subsequently attacked Japanese bases and shipping in the Marianas, Palaus, Formosa, Okinawa and the Philippines. Although held in reserve on 20 June 1944, Bombing 15 had numerous other opportunities to engage the enemy, and was credited with sinking or damaging a record tonnage of Japanese merchant and combat ships.

4

SB2C-1C white 68 of VB-1, USS *Yorktown*, June 1944

Bombing Squadron One served aboard *Yorktown* (CV-10) from May to August 1944, with a hectic two weeks of June in the Marianas and the Bonins. In the Battle of the Philippine Sea, *Yorktown* sent 14 Helldivers against the Japanese carriers and lost nine aircraft but no crews. Eight SB2Cs landed in the ocean from fuel exhaustion and another crashed aboard *Cabot* (CVL-28) and had to be jettisoned. Bombing One returned to combat aboard *Bennington* (CV-20) in June 1945, remaining in combat until the cessation of hostilities in August. By then the squadron had re-equipped with SB2C-4Es bearing the 'TT' tail code letters.

5

SB2C-1C BuNo 00334, white 48 of VB-2, USS *Hornet*, 20 June 1944

Assigned to squadron flight (operations) officer, Lt H L Buell, BuNo 00334 was a replacement aircraft that Buell flew only twice. The first time was from the escort carrier *Copahee* (CVE-12) to *Hornet* (CV-12) on 14 June, whilst the second, and last, time w was on the strike against the Japanese Mobile Fleet six days later. On that occasion Buell led his division in an attack against IJNS *Zuikaku*. Wounded in the action, he navigated back to the US task force and crash-landed aboard USS *Lexington*. His radioman-gunner was ACRM/2c W D Lakey. The aircraft number 48 was repeated in black on the landing gear doors. While VB-2 aircraft were nominally assigned to specific crews, names apparently were not applied.

6

SB2C-1C BuNo 21211, white 73 of VB-2, USS *Hornet*, 20 June 1944

Lt(jg) D S Stear and ARM2/c W E Redman flew this Helldiver in the 'mission beyond darkness' on 20 June 1944. Like Lt Buell, Stear found his way to the task force flagship, USS *Lexington*, and crashed aboard. Radioman Redman was killed in the accident and the aircraft was jettisoned. Of the 14 Helldivers VB-2 launched on the mission, two returned safely, landing aboard *Enterprise* and *Bunker Hill*. One was shot down, eight made water landings, and three were scrapped with extensive damage.

7

SB2C-1C BuNo 18358, white 24 of VB-8, USS *Bunker Hill*, 20 June 1944

Bombing Squadron Eight succeeded VB-17 in *Bunker Hill*, beginning in March 1944. The high point of the eight-month cruise was the First Battle of the Philippine Sea, fought on 19-20 June. On the

20th, VB-8 attacked the light carrier *Chiyoda*, which sustained bomb damage. Lt(jg) W P Huntsmen and ARM2/c E A Houstoun flew this Helldiver in the dusk attack. Trying to get back to *Bunker Hill*, they ran out of fuel and ditched near Task Force 58. The crew was subsequently rescued by the destroyer USS *Miller* (DD-535) during the task force's extensive search and rescue operation.

8

SB2C-1C BuNo 18331, white 20 of VB-8, USS *Bunker Hill*, 20 June 1944

Forced into a water landing on 20 June 1944, Lt(jg) W F Pilcher and ARM2/c R B Bailey were rescued by the destroyer USS *Izard* (DD-589). Bombing Eight lost 11 of the 12 aircraft despatched on the late afternoon mission against the Japanese Mobile Fleet, the sole survivor recovering aboard light carrier *Cabot* (CVL-28). Two Helldivers and their crews were lost in combat and eight made ditchings, with one crew not rescued.

9

SB2C-3 white 75 of VB-19, USS *Lexington*, July 1944

Relieving one of the last two SBD squadrons in Task Force 58, VB-19 was determined to prove the worth of the Helldiver. Lt Cdr R McGowan's squadron subsequently demonstrated that the SB2C-3 had become a reliable dive-bomber, winning the confidence of Vice Adm Mitscher who rode *Lexington* (CV-16) as commander of the fast carriers. Rare in having no air group symbol, CVG-19's squadrons used a variety of markings, the most distinctive being the bombers' oversize white block letters on the tail. Pilots and gunners' ranks and names were stencilled in white below the respective cockpits. The Hellcats of VF-19 used stencilled numbers behind the cockpit while Torpedo 19's TBM Avengers displayed an inverted triangle.

10

SB2C-3 white 54 of VB-14, USS *Wasp*, August 1944

A small white triangle on the vertical stabiliser denoted *Wasp* (CV-18) squadrons. Air Group 14, established in September 1943, and had only four months of work-ups before boarding *Wasp*. Bombing 14, which flew combat between May and November 1944, was heavily hit in the 'mission beyond darkness' of 20 June. When false reports drew Air Group 14 south of the main track toward the Japanese carriers, the bombing squadron commander decided to attack enemy oilers instead, and sank two. However, VB-14 lost all but one of 12 aircraft on the mission, with four crews killed in combat or ditchings.

11

SB2C-3 white 30 of VB-13, USS *Franklin*, 7 August 1944

Similar to VB-19, VB-13's markings were generally limited to large numbers on the vertical stabiliser and rudder. On many aircraft the unit insignia was displayed just behind the engine accessory section. VB-13 was embarked in *Franklin* (CV-13) from July to October 1944, but the deployment was prematurely ended when the ship sustained *kamikaze* damage off the Philippines on 30 October. By then the standard complement of carrier-based SB2Cs had been reduced from 36 to 24 to make more room for fighters.

12

SB2C-3 white 22 of VB-7, USS *Hancock*, 13 October 1944

Often mistaken for a horseshoe, *Hancock's* (CV-19) air group emblem was a stencilled Greek letter Omega. Bombing 7, which flew from 'Hanna' between September 1944 and January 1945, had other distinctive markings – a narrow white band on the engine cowling, and individual names on several of its aircraft. Apparently all were rendered in white script, as shown on '22' – christened *Satan's Angel*. This SB2C-3 carries a twin .30-cal gun pack under each wing, a weapon intended for close air support but seldom employed.

13

SB2C-3 white 61 of VB-18, USS *Intrepid*, 25 October 1944

Although only in combat from September to November 1944, *Intrepid's* (CV-11) Bombing Squadron 18 saw a great deal of action. Two days of particularly intense operations came on 24 and 25 October during strikes against Japanese surface forces in the Sibuyan Sea and against remaining enemy carriers off the north-east coast of Luzon. VB-18 contributed to sinking the super battleship *Musashi* on the 24th, but lost five SB2Cs in the process. The air group insignia throughout this period was a white cross at the tip of the vertical stabiliser. Suicide aircraft forced the carrier's withdrawl on 25 November.

14

SB2C-3 white 2 of VB-4, USS *Bunker Hill*, 13 November 1944

Bombing Four was one of the few Navy squadrons with combat against both major Axis powers. Flying SBD-5s, VB-4 attacked German-controlled shipping in Norway while embarked in *Ranger* (CV-4) in late 1943. Then, newly-qualified in SB2Cs, the squadron went to the Pacific to fight Imperial Japan. Flying a split tour, VB-4 relieved Bombing 8 in *Bunker Hill* for a short period in November 1944, then replaced Bombing 15 aboard *Essex*, remaining until March 1945. While in *Bunker Hill*, VB-4 used this variation on the bars above the aircraft number. Aboard *Essex*, the same white band around the tail was retained from Air Group 15.

15
SB2C-3 black 3 of VB-20, USS *Enterprise*, 24 November 1944
Another squadron flying from two carriers in one deployment was Bombing 20, embarked in *Enterprise* from August to November 1944. The white triangle on the tail had a black number superimposed, which was repeated on the cowling as well. Transferred to *Lexington*, Air Group 20 remained in 'Lady Lex' until January 1945. Part way through the cruise VB-20's skipper, Cdr R E Riera, was moved to *Hornet* to assume command of Air Group 11, where his first flight in a Hellcat was made while at sea!

16
SB2C-3 white 10 of VB-80, USS *Ticonderoga*, late 1944
'Tico's' original air group included Bombing Squadron 80, which entered combat during the Philippines campaign in November 1944. Remaining aboard until January 1945, the air group then transferred to *Hancock* in time for the fast carrier strikes on Japan in mid-February, and departed for the US in March. *Ticonderoga's* slanting line on the tail is repeated under the port wing – a common practice by late 1944.

17
SB2C-4 white 6 of VB-80, USS *Ticonderoga*, late 1944
Bearing identical markings to Number 10, this VB-80 aircraft has the overall gloss dark blue colour scheme standardised in 1944. The front half of the propeller spinner is painted white. In December the organisation of carrier air groups was altered, with SB2Cs reduced from 24 to 15 aircraft per embarked squadron – a concession to the increasing threat of Japanese suicide tactics which raised F6F strength from 54 to 73 Hellcats.

18
SB2C-4 white 114 of VB-3, USS *Yorktown*, late 1944
Among the most famous bombing squadrons in the US Navy, VB-3 adopted its 'leaping panther' in 1934. Ten years later the emblem still adorned Bombing Three aircraft, as this Helldiver demonstrates. After flying SBDs at Midway and Guadalcanal, VB-3 converted to SB2Cs and took them to the Western Pacific from October 1944 to March 1945. By then, *Yorktown's* emblem was a diagon-

ally-painted rear half of the vertical fin and rudder, with three-digit numbers on the tail and fuselage.

19
SB2C-3 white 16 of 4th Marine Aircraft Wing, Marshall Islands, March 1945
The 4th Marine Aircraft Wing was responsible for control of Japanese-occupied islands in the Marshalls group during 1944-45. Several 'Flying Leatherneck' squadrons had SB2Cs in that period, but this aircraft is probably from VMSB-151. The squadron was based on Engebi Island, and at the time it was the only operational Marine unit flying Helldivers in the area, although it also retained several SBD-5s. The headquarters squadron of Marine Air Group 13 at Majuro also had 24 SB2C-4s for utility and proficiency flying.

20
SB2C-3 white 105 of VB-9, USS *Lexington*, 2 March 1945
Air Group Nine began its second wartime cruise while embarked in *Lexington* during February and March 1945. Previousl,y Bombing Nine had flown Dauntlesses from *Essex* in 1943-44, receiving its first Helldivers (SBW-3s) at NAS Pasco, Washington, in September 1944. The major actions of the 1945 deployment were the Tokyo strikes and the invasion of Iwo Jima. However, the group transferred to *Yorktown* from March until June – toward the end of the Okinawa campaign.

21
SB2C-4E white 95 of VB-82, USS *Bennington*, February 1945
Air Group 82 was formed in April 1944, with the bombing squadron based at Wildwood, New Jersey. Originally equipped with 36 SB2C-1Cs, VB-82 had embarked in *Bennington* (CV-20) with 15 -4Es by the end of January 1945. With its AN/APS-4 radar carried on the hardpoint beneath the wing, this aircraft flew from 'Benny' between February and June 1945. That part of the war encompassed the Japanese home islands raids, and support of the landings at Iwo Jima and Okinawa.

22
SB2C-4E white 15 of VB-12, USS *Randolph*, February 1945
Air Group 12's first combat was over Japan itself during the 16-17 February strikes upon the Tokyo Plain. Among the most distinctive markings carried by any Helldiver squadron of the period, VB-12 SB2Cs bore the horizontal tail stripes and unusual placement of individual aircraft numbers well forward on the fuselage, just behind the engine cowling. By this time most air groups had adopted three-digit side numbers.

23
SB2C-4 white 80 of VB-85, USS *Shangri-La*, 3 June 1945
In combat during the last five months of hostilities, Air Group 85 began operations at Okinawa and was heavily involved in attacks against Japan itself. The first air group of the new *Shangri-La* (CV-38) applied this dazzling lightning bolt to its aircraft with side number on the rudder and engine cowling. The ship's unconventional name had originated in President Roosevelt's quip following the April 1942 Doolittle raid from *Hornet* (CV-8) – he commented that it looked as if the B-25s had taken off from the mythical 'Shangri-La' as featured in British author James Hilton's 1934 novel, *Lost Horizon*.

24
SB2C-4E white 205 of VB-84, USS *Bunker Hill*, 18 March 1945
Generically called 'The Wolf Gang', Air Group 84 was among several fast carrier units that broke into combat during the home islands attacks of February 1945. Also involved in close air support at Okinawa and the *Yamato* strike in April, VB-84 lost all 15 of its aircraft in a skillfully executed *kamikaze* attack against *Bunker Hill* on 11 May. After replacing heavy casualties, the squadron was preparing to redeploy when the war ended in September.

25
SB2C-4 white 207 of VB-83, USS *Essex*, 1 April 1945
An early-production SB2C-4 in tricolour markings, this Bombing 83 aircraft flew from *Essex* at the start of the Okinawa battle on April Fools' Day 1945. A week later came the attack on the Japanese task force built around the super battleship *Yamato*, sunk north-east of Okinawa on the 7th. Bombing 83 found the SB2C-4 an improvement over previous Helldiver models, and was still engaged in combat on the last day of hostilities, 15 August.

26
SB2C-4E white 203 of VB-87, USS *Ticonderoga*, 6 June 1945
Bombing 87 began combat operations from *Ticonderoga* in May 1945, sporting distinctive inverted triangles on the tail and wings. As frequently applied during this period, the upper starboard and lower port wings repeated the 'G' symbol for easier recognition from all aspects in flight. This aircraft was lost in the carrier pattern on 6 June 1945, but the pilot and radioman-gunner escaped before the Helldiver sank.

27
SB2C-4E white 209 of VB-87, USS *Ticonderoga*, 25 July 1945
Following the air group/ship identification change of 10 July, VB-87 aircraft exchanged their triangles for the letter 'V' during the final weeks of World War 2. Number 208 sustained heavy battle damage during a mission over Japan on 25 July, but returned to *Ticonderoga* and safely got aboard. Note that in contrast to Number 203's all-white spinner, Number 208's is half and half.

28
SB2C-4E white 318 of VB-83, USS *Essex*, 30 July '45
By July 1945, VB-83 was equipped wholly with SB2C-4s and -4Es. This example of the latter exhibits some hastily-applied paint, as the new 'F' designation replaced the previous *Essex* 'double diamond' seen in profile number 25. Visible overspray of the letter 'F' indicates that aircraft 318 had received hasty attention—an understandable situation during the press of combat operations.

29
SB2C-4E white 8 of VB-16, USS *Randolph*, 30 July 1945
Bombing 16 was one of the fleet's last two SBD squadrons, leaving *Lexington* in July 1944. A year later VB-16 was back in combat, flying Helldivers from *Randolph* in missions against the defuelled Japanese fleet at Kure and elsewhere. As noted with VB-84, the unusual placement of individual aircraft numbers saw them applied well forward on the fuselage, with additional smaller numbers on the cowling and vertical stabiliser.

30
SB2C-4E white 82 of VB-85, USS *Shangri-La*, 11 August 1945
Shangri-La's dramatic lightning bolt (see profile 23) was replaced with the identification letter 'Z' in July 1945. Bombing 85 was still aboard 'Shang' on VJ-Day, but the air group was decommissioned on 27 September, barely three weeks after the Japanese had formally surrendered in Tokyo Bay. At that time nine Helldiver squadrons were operating with the fast carrier task force, all equipped with SB2C-4s or -4Es.

31
SB2C-4E white 114 of VB-150, USS *Lake Champlain*, August 1945
Formed on the East Coast in January 1945, Air Group 150 was assigned to the new *Essex*-class carrier *Lake Champlain* (CV-39). One of the few air groups to escape the 10 July change to letters rather than 'G' symbols, CVG-150's emblem was a stylised inverted 'L' on the tail and wing surfaces.

The air group was disestablished on 2 November without ever having had the opportunity to complete a full-length deployment. Both VB-152 and -153 were also based on the East Coast, each with 15 or more SB2C-5s, whilst VB-151 had yet to receive aircraft in the Pacific Northwest.

32

SB2C-5 white 82 of VB-10, USS *Intrepid*, September 1945

Bombing 10 was one of the most experienced carrier squadrons in the Navy by 1945. With two previous SBD cruises in *Enterprise* in 1942-43 and 1944, VB-10 exchanged Dauntlesses for Helldivers in September 1944 and deployed aboard *Intrepid* (CV-11) in March 1945. Operations were conducted against Okinawa and Japan, but suicide damage to 'Evil I' on 16 April forced her back to the West Coast, and she did not return to the Western Pacific until shortly before the cease-fire in mid-August. The only additional combat seen by VB-10 in that short period was a 'warm-up' strike on Wake Island.

33

SB2C-5 white 8 of the Victory Squadron, October 1945

Also called 'The Navy's Flying Might', the Victory Squadron was a composite unit with SB2C-5s, F6F-5s, F7F-1s, F4U-4s and TBM-3s, plus an assortment of support aircraft including a captured Zero and 'Kate'. Led by Lt Cdr W E Eder, the unit was comprised of combat-experienced aviators whose records were emblazoned on the side of their aircraft. 'VS-8' had 36 bombs representing mission markers, with the pilot's name stencilled below the cockpit. Its usual pilot was probably Lt(jg) C B Stafford. 'The Flying Might' programme toured the US from October 1945 to January 1946, raising $18(US) million in public contributions through the performance of airshows across the country. Photographic evidence indicates that 'VS 1-3' were F6Fs, '4-6' F4Us, '7-9' SB2Cs, '10-12' TBMs and '13-15' F7Us.

FIGURE PLATES

1

Lt Cdr Richard S McGowan, CO of VB-19 aboard *Lexington* (CV-16) in October 1944. He is wearing standard issue US Navy officer's khaki shirt and trousers, with badges of rank affixed to his shirt collar. McGowan's helmet is a lightweight tropical issue AN-H-15, combined with late-pattern Polaroid B-8 goggles. He has QMC-issue 'Boondocker' boots on his feet, and his flying gear is completed with the addition of a N2885 life preserver

2

Enlisted radioman/gunner in the Pacific in 1944. Attired in an enlisted man's work shirt and dungarees, this individual is wearing an M40 flying helmet with Wilson Mk II goggles. Aside from his N2885, he also has a QAS parachute and an AN-R2 (seat pack) raft. His gloves are lightweight issue, he is carrying a .38-cal revolver in his waist webbing and he has 'boondockers' on his feet.

3

Lt Bob Wood, flight (operations) officer of VB-17, is seen in mid-1943 whilst based at NAS Norfolk, Virginia. He is wearing the 'Garrison' cap and trousers of the green naval aviator's service uniform – note the badge of rank and aviation branch insignia on his cap. Wood has a standard A-2 flight jacket on, adorned with a flier's brevet and his name on the breast. He is carrying a N2885 life preserver and cloth helmet, whilst his shoes and gloves are civilian pattern.

BIBLIOGRAPHY

Buell, Harold L *Dauntless Helldivers*. Orion, New York, 1991
Bowers, Peter M *Curtiss Aircraft*. Putnam, New York, 1973
DeChant, John A *Devilbirds*. Harper Brothers, New York, 1947
Forsyth, John F *Hell Divers*. Motorbooks, Osceola, WI, 1991
Hoyt, Edwin P *McCampbell's Heroes*. Van Nostrand Reinhold, New York, 1983
Morison, Samuel E *History of US Navy Operations in World War II*. Volume XII: *Leyte*. Little-Brown Co, Boston, 1963
Volume XIV: *Victory in the Pacific*. Little-Brown Co, Boston, 1964
Olds, Robert *Helldiver Squadron*. Dodd, Mead Co, New York, 1945
Polmar, Norman *Aircraft Carriers*. Doubleday, Garden City, 1969
Sherrod, Robert *History of Marine Corps Aviation in World War II*. Presidio Press, San Rafael, California, 1980
Spurr, Russell *A Glorious Way to Die: the Kamikaze Mission of the Battleship Yamato*. Newmarket Press, New York, 1981
Tillman, Barrett *Carrier Battle in the Philippine Sea*. Phalanx Pub. Co, St. Paul, 1994
The Dauntless Dive Bomber of World War II Naval Institute Press, Annapolis, Maryland, 1979
US Navy Monthly Location and Allowance Reports of Aircraft, 1943-1945. Bureau of Aeronautics, Washington, DC.
US Navy *The USS Bunker Hill - November 1943 to November 1944*, Department of the Navy, Washington, DC, 1945
Wagner, Ray *American Combat Planes*. Doubleday, New York, 1968
Winters, T Hugh *Skipper: Confessions of a Fighter Squadron Commander 1943-44*. Champlin Press, Mesa, AZ, 1985
Y'Blood, William T *Red Sun Setting: the Battle of the Philippine Sea*. Naval Institute Press, Annapolis, 1981